Lands of our Ancestors

Books 1-3

Teacher's Guides

© 2016-2023
Tribal Eye Productions
P.O. Box 1123 / Santa Ynez, CA 93460
www.LandsOfOurAncestors.com

© 2016-2023 Tribal Eye Productions
ISBN 978-1-7352003-9-2
All Rights Reserved

TABLE OF CONTENTS

1. BOOK ONE TEACHER'S GUIDE — p. 5
   - Overview of the Chumash People — p. 7
   - The Chumash in Historic Times — p. 9
   - Images of Chumash Traditional Life — p. 10
   - Accuracy of Events Portrayed — p. 13
   - Information Sources on the Chumash People — p. 15
   - Information Sources on California Missions — p. 15
   - Chapter Questions & Answers /Words — p. 16
   - Student Projects — p. 48

2. BOOK 2 TEACHER'S GUIDE — p. 55
   - Introduction to the Teacher's Guide — p. 57
   - Fourth Grade HSS Standards — p. 58
   - Overview – Mexican Rancho Period — p. 59
   - Images Depicting the Era — p. 63
   - Accuracy of Events Portrayed — p. 67
   - Information Sources on the Chumash — p. 69
   - Information Sources on the Ranchos — p. 69
   - Characters & Relationships — p. 71
   - Timeline of Events — p. 72
   - Chapter Q & A / Words to Know — p. 75
   - Student Projects — p. 101

TABLE OF CONTENTS, *continued*

3. BOOK 3 TEACHER'S GUIDE	p. 107
Introduction to the Teacher Guide	p. 109
Fourth Grade HSS Standards	p. 110
Overview of Gold Rush Period and Early California Statehood	p. 112
Accuracy of Events Portrayed	p. 114
Images Depicting the Era	p. 115
Geographical Locations in Book Three	p. 118
Information Sources on the Chumash Gold Rush and Early Statehood	p. 119
Characters & Relationships	p. 120
Timeline of Events	p. 121
Chapter Questions & Answers	p. 125
Words to Know for Each Chapter	
Student Projects	p. 146
Acknowledgments	p. 148

Lands of our Ancestors-Book 1
Teacher's Guide

Developed by
Cathleen Chilcote Wallace
and Gary Robinson

Lands of Our Ancestors
Teachers Guide Introduction

This Teachers Guide is designed to enrich teaching Lands of Our Ancestors- Book 1 across the curriculum. The guide begins with an overview of the Chumash people before European contact. This information will provide the teacher with important background information about the Chumash people in pre-Columbian California and can be used to introduce the book. This is followed by a summary of the Chumash in historic times up to the present where the cultural revitalization work of present day Chumash people is also highlighted. In addition, there are three pages of images of traditional Chumash houses, foods, tools, a ceremonial leader, and a hunter. These images help illustrate the story. At this point the guide also includes a section that validates the accuracy of the events portrayed in the story and a list of sources of further information on the Chumash and the historic missions.

The second section of the guide contains "Questions, Answers, and Words to Know" for each chapter of Lands of Our Ancestors. The questions can be used in teacher directed class discussions, small group discussions, or as written work. The variety of questions in each chapter align with The Six Levels of Questioning: knowledge, comprehension, application, analysis, synthesis, evaluation. Answers are provided for all chapter questions. New vocabulary, including Chumash words, are found in each chapter's "Words to Know" page.

Finally, to extend the learning after the book is completed, the guide includes eight project choices to engage students. The projects are designed to meet the needs of the diverse learners found in most classrooms. Each project meets a specific fourth grade History-Social Science Content Standard for California Public Schools. The standard is listed with each project.

Students who complete reading the story, discuss or write responses to the questions, and learn the new vocabulary words will meet a variety of the fourth grade California Common Core State Standards in reading, writing, and language.

Overview of the Chumash People Before European Contact

The Chumash Indians have lived along the southcentral California coast and nearby inland regions for at least 13,000 years. Their prehistoric territory stretched from Malibu in the south to Morro Bay and San Luis Obispo in the north, and from the Channel Islands in the west to the inland areas around Cuyama, CA. Over time, the language of these autonomous groups evolved into eight different versions of the Chumash language, related to one another in a way similar to how Latin, Italian and Spanish are related to each other.

The Chumash way of life depended on the natural world around them. This world provided everything the people needed for food, clothing, shelter, medicine, tools and weapons. Because they lived so close to nature, the Chumash had very detailed knowledge about the wild plants, animals, and minerals that they relied on.

They knew how to use more than 150 different plants for food, medicine and ceremonial applications. These included oak trees for acorns, chia seeds from sage plants, plus the nuts, seeds, bulbs, roots and leaves of many other plants. However, acorns were *the* most important plant food for the Chumash and most California Indians. Acorns are poisonous to humans unless they are first ground into a fine meal, washed (leached) at least three times and then cooked. This makes a filling, thick brown mush somewhat like oatmeal, often eaten with more flavorful foods like dried fish or venison (deer meat). Pine nuts were also an important food. Trips to pine tree forests at distant higher elevations were part of the Chumash annual food-gathering cycle.

They were skillful hunters of wild games such as deer, antelope, rabbits, birds and seals. They also enjoyed a wide variety of fish and shellfish that came from the ocean and rivers in the area. Salmon of the Santa Ynez River was one of their favorites.

The Chumash home was built of Tule reeds spread over frames made of willow branches. This round half-dome house, called an *ap* (op) included a small fire pit at the center with a small smoke hole in the roof. Sizes of these homes varied greatly depending on the size of the family living in one. A village was often made up of rows of aps and included an enclosed area for religious activities, acorn storage facilities, a playing field for sporting games, and a sweat house where daily hot sweat baths were taken for both cleansing and healing.

Their religious beliefs included an understanding of certain supernatural powers that resided in the natural world, including the sky world. Movements of the sun, moon and stars revealed hidden meanings to the tribal spiritual leaders who keep an ever-watchful eye on the sky. These people were part of the twelve-member council called the *antap* (ontop) that provided leadership and guidance to members of the community. Each major village had its own council of twelve, which included the local village chief.

This way of life was developed and practiced for thousands of years uninterrupted until the arrival of Spanish priest, soldiers and settlers in the 1700s.

The Chumash in Historical Times

Explorers sailing on Spanish ships visited the California coast a few times in the 1500s and 1600s, but it wasn't until 1769 that Gaspar de Portola led an expedition to the region to establish permanent settlements here. This was a combined religious and military effort to ensure that Spain had firm colonial control of the area. Franciscan priests were charged with the duty of creating Catholic missions to convert Indians to Christianity, and soldiers were assigned the duty of maintaining order within these communities. Their ultimate goal was to add more territory to the Spanish empire.

Starting in San Diego, a total of twenty-one missions were established and operated, but these institutions were more like slave plantations than outposts of the Christian faith. Indians who came to the missions were forced to work daily to build all the buildings, raise and slaughter cattle, plant and harvest crops, prepare and cook food, weave cloth for clothing, and perform all the tasks needed to maintain a Spanish settlement. If Indians failed to do their work or tried to run away because of the way they were treated, soldiers on horseback were sent to capture them and bring them back. Then the Indians were often beaten with whips as punishment or locked in shackles to prevent them from trying again.

Five missions were built in Chumash territory, and due to the spread of European diseases and abusive slave labor practices, the tribal population shrank by at least 80% during the sixty-year mission period. This was true of the Native American population all over the California region.

The Indians that survived did learn domestic skills like how to plant and harvest crops, ride horses, tend cattle, cook European foods, use tools, and wash clothes, but in the years following the end of the mission era, that's all they were allowed to do. They became the underpaid servants of the Mexican landowners who took over the area after Mexico won independence from Spain.

And Indians fared no better under American rule after 1848 when the U.S. took the Southwest from Mexico in war. Congress then declined to ratify treaties with California tribes, and the newly created state government passed laws stripping all rights from indigenous people.

However, today, the Chumash people, particularly the tiny Santa Ynez Band of Chumash, have begun to rebuild their tribal nation. Using revenues from their federally authorized casino and resort, they are providing education and health services to their people. Instruction in tribal history, culture and language are allowing new generations of Chumash to forge a new, hopeful future.

In fact, tribes all over California have been able to begin regaining lost cultures and re-learning nearly lost languages in the 21st century. These losses were directly caused by the priests and soldiers who founded and operated the Spanish missions and were determined to convert California's Native Americans into Spanish colonial citizens at any cost.

Examples of Chumash Traditional Life

Chumash House - Ap (op)

Chumash Village Scene

Examples of Chumash Traditional Life-p.2

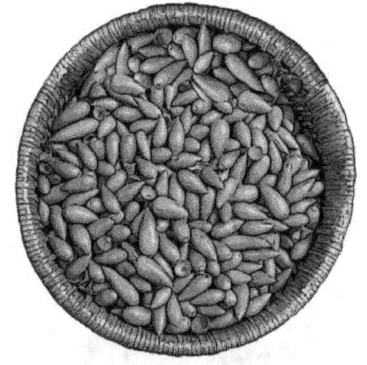

Acorns: A major food for many California Indians

Acorn grinding stone

Salmon: an important food for the Chumash

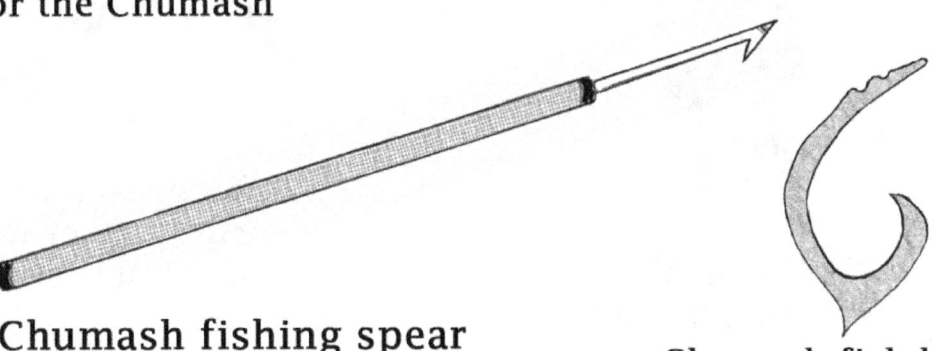

Chumash fishing spear

Chumash fish hook

Examples of Chumash Traditional Life - p.3

Chumash
Ceremonial Leader

Chumash hunter
wearing a deer decoy
head and skin

Accuracy of Events Portrayed in Lands of our Ancestors

As stated in the "Note to Teachers and Parents" at the beginning to Lands of our Ancestors, this work of historical fiction depicts what *might* have happened when a village of Chumash Indian people encountered the Spanish padres and soldiers who came to California to establish religious missions and create colonial outposts in the area. The missions, presidios and settlements they established all relied on forced Indian labor to operate, a fact that has been hidden from public view far too long.

Spanish colonial Franciscan priests, led by Junipero Serra, ultimately forced Indians to build twenty-one of these institutions between San Diego and Sonoma, impacting the lives of at least 100,000 indigenous people from forty or more different tribes. The California Native population was depleted by about 80% as a result of the mission approach to converting Indians not only to Christianity, but also to "civilized" Spanish citizens.

What happens to the Chumash characters in Lands of our Ancestors is typical of what may have happened to all the tribal people who came into contact with any of the missions built on their ancestral lands. The scenes in the book such as the intense flogging of Indians who attempted to escape and depictions of daily schedules and forced labor are soundly rooted in historical research.

The books listed in the bibliography include some of the sources of that historical research. Below is a summary of the research on the punishments used by the priests against Indians who didn't follow mission rules.

Junipero Serra's mandate from the King of Spain was to educate the Indians of California and then release them. Instead, Serra took it upon himself to effectively imprison them for life and use the Native Americans as forced labor… The mission Indians, called neophytes by the friars, had terrible, sadistic punishments inflicted on them by the Franciscans… One distinguished visitor to Mission Carmel was shocked at the fetid squalor in which the Indians were forced to live. Bedraggled Indians, some in shackles and stocks, were being walked to a work site accompanied by guards who swung whips to ensure their staying together. The sight, he wrote in his log, was no different than the slave plantations he'd visited in the Caribbean. He described the policies of the Franciscans toward the mission Indians as *reprehensible, adding they were <u>beating the Indians for violations that in Europe would be considered insignificant</u>.*

By far, one of the cruelest incidents was described in 1825 by Robert Forbes, the master of a New England trading ship. He visited Mission San Francisco and was shocked by the <u>savagery</u> of the friars. He took note of the "Christianizing Padres" who converted the Indians by sending gauchos and rancheros into the field to catch them with a lasso. He said the friars then branded the Indians with a hot branding iron shaped like a cross.

At both Mission San Gabriel and Mission San Luis Rey, the Indians faced the twisted wrath of Friar Jose Zalvidea. A visiting rancher noted the padre's penchant for punishment including his cruelty toward women who suffered miscarriages. Instead of offering comfort, the friar ordered them to be <u>lashed</u> for 15 days, their heads shaved, and <u>irons</u> bolted around their ankles for 3 months. Each bereaved mother also had to stand every Sunday on the steps of the church <u>hold a hideous painted wooden child</u> in her arms.

-Source: <u>A Cross of Thorns</u> by Elias Castillo.

Due to their "animal-like natures," California Indians often made mistakes or misbehaved even when they had been told the rules. Like good fathers everywhere, the padres believed in firm discipline and consequences; usually this meant <u>flogging</u>, but sometimes other kinds of corporal punishment were used. In a long letter of complaint to the King of Spain, one South American Indian provided a <u>catalog of Spanish punishments</u> for Indians that included <u>flogging</u>, <u>hanging upside down</u>, and being <u>put in stocks</u>. Franciscans Fathers used these and other disciplinary actions to help "civilize" California Indians and turn them into good Christians and loyal Spanish subjects. These included those already mentioned plus <u>beating with a cudgel</u>, <u>whipping with a cat-o-nine tails</u> and <u>hobbling with an ankle hobble</u>.

-Source: <u>Bad Indians</u> by Deborah A. Miranda.

Sources on the Chumash People:

1. California's Chumash Indians, A Project of the Santa Barbara Museum of Natural History; EZ Nature Books; 1992, Revised Edition 2002.

2. The Chumash, Seafarers of the Pacific Coast; Karen Bush Gibson; Capstone Press, 2004.

3. "The Samala People" (DVD); produced by the Santa Ynez Band of Chumash Indians; Available from the tribe's Culture Department; 805-688-7997.

4. Bad Indians: A Tribal Memoir; Deborah A. Miranda; Heyday, 2013.

5. Samala-English Dictionary-A Guide to the Samala Language of the Ineseno Chumash People; Santa Ynez Band of Chumash Indians with Richard Applegate, PhD; 2007.

6. Website: www.sbnature.org/research/anthro/chumash/intro.htm (Chumash section of the Santa Barbara Museum of Natural History's website)

7. Website: www.santaynezchumash.org/history.html (The Santa Ynez Band of Chumash Indians official website)

8. Wikipedia Website: https://en.wikipedia.org/wiki/Chumash_people

Sources on California Missions:

1. A Cross of Thorns-The Enslavement of California's Indians by the Spanish Missions; Elias Castillo; Craven Street Books; 2015.

2. Junipero Serra, the Vatican, and Enslavement Theology; Daniel Fogel; Ism Press; 1988.

3. The Other Slavery-The Uncovered Story of Indian Enslavement in America; Andres Resendez; Houghton Mifflin Harcourt; 2016.

4. http:// www.whenturtlesfly.blogspot.com - Deborah Miranda's blog on California Indians and the Native experience in the missions.

5. Website: http://www.missionscalifornia.com; hosted by the California Missions Resource Center. (NOTE: This is a one-sided presentation of facts about the missions and gives no indications that there were negative aspects to mission life for California's Indians.)

6. Website: http://www.huffingtonpost.com/the-zinn-education-project/lying-to-children-about-t_b_6924346.html. (NOTE: This article on the Internet points out the blatant stereotypes found in most material used to teach the "Mission Unit."

Lands of Our Ancestors

Chapter 1 - Preparations
Questions

1. Describe the main characters Kilik and Tuhuy. Compare and contrast the boys. What is their relationship?

2. What is the game that Kilik and Tuhuy are playing? Describe the game; how is it played? What is the function of the game and why does Kilik practice with such determination?

3. When the story begins, what time of the year is it? Explain the importance of the season. What do you imagine the mood of the village is?

4. What did you learn about the Chumash people of the Place of River Turtles in Chapter 1? List three facts from the story.

Answers

1. Kilik is twelve years old. His name means "Sparrow Hawk". He is confident, determined, athletic, and a leader. Kilik is eager to use his hunting skills to bring food to the village.

   Tuhuy is eleven years old. His name means "Rain". He is a "thinker" and is determined to improve his skills although he does not believe he will ever be as skilled as Kilik.

   Kilik and Tuhuy are cousins and best friends who are always together. They are both kind, obedient, and respectful to their families and elders. They work together, each using their special abilities to complete a task or solve a problem.

2. Kilik and Tuhuy play the traditional hoop-and-pole game. One boy rolls a small hoop on the ground and the other boy throws a long spear-like pole through the hoop. The game helps boys develop their hunting skills. Kilik is determined to have sharp skills for his first hunt.

3. The story begins at the end of summer. It is the time for Hutash, the yearly harvest festival. Hutash is also the name for Mother Earth. The mood in the village is probably excited, busy, and thoughtful. (Accept other appropriate responses.)

4. Facts from Chapter 1 about the Chumash people:
   - The Chumash people live in villages, in homes made of tule reeds, with leaders and extended family members.
   - Family groups work together and help each other.
   - The Chumash people (and all native people) respect Mother Earth.
   - Chumash children are expected to work but also play games and have toys.
   - Traditions are important to the Chumash people.
   - Dances, songs, and stories are important to the Chumash culture.
   - (Accept other appropriate answers.)

Words to Know

Chumash Names and Words:

Kilik (Kee-leek): Sparrow Hawk; young boy
Tuhuy (Too-hooy): Rain; young boy, Kilik's cousin
Salapay (Sal-uh-pie): To lift or raise up; Tuhuy's father, Kilik's uncle
Solomol (Soh-loh-mole): To straighten and arrow; Kilik's father, Tuhuy's uncle
Wonono (Wo-no-no): Small Owl; Kilik's mother
Yol (rhymes with pole): Bluebird; Tuhuy's mother
Stuk (Rhymes with Luke): Ladybug; Kilik's sister
Kimi (Kee-mee): To repeat, do over; Stuk's nickname

Hutash: Chumash harvest ceremony; Chumash name for Mother Earth

Chumash: The Chumash are native people of the south-central region of California who have lived in the area for at least 9,000 years. The people lived in small self-governing groups spread over several thousand square miles. Different Chumash languages were spoken in the communities. In this book, the tribe lives in the Santa Ynez Valley and speaks Samala Chumash. Other Chumash groups are known as Barbareño and Ventureño.

Words to Know
(in order of appearance in the story)

ancestor: a person related to you who lived a long time ago; your grandmother's grandmother and anyone who lived before her

hurl: to throw with great force

thrust: to push something suddenly in a specific direction

cease: stop, quit, discontinue

quiver: a case for holding arrows, usually made from animal skin

endurance: the ability to keep doing something difficult, unpleasant, or painful for a long time

ceremony: an event with special traditions, actions, or word

harvest: a season when food is gathered from the land

gathering: a time when people come together as a group, especially for a festive occasion

Tule reeds: tall, green reeds with spongy stems

acorn granary: a very large, round basket-like receptacle made from willow to store acorns

scornful: a very strong feeling of no respect for someone

tradition: a way of behaving or a belief that has been established for a long time

shell bead money: strands of beads made from small disks shaped from the Olivella shell

trickster: someone who uses their intelligence to play tricks on others and sometimes breaks the rules

Chapter 2 - House of the Moon
Questions

1. The day of Kilik's first hunting trip finally arrives. Explain why this is such an important event for him. Can you imagine how he feels as he sets out with his father?

2. In addition to hunting skills, what does Kilik's father teach him? Why do you think this is important?

3. Using evidence (information) from the story, describe the area where the tribe's village is built. Can you think of a reason why the village is built in that location?

4. How would you describe the special relationship the Chumash people (all native people) have with Mother Earth?

5. The double halos around the moon are an example of foreshadowing. What change do you think is coming for the Chumash? Support your prediction with evidence from the story.

Answers

1. Kilik's first hunting trip is important to him because he wants to prove that he can provide food for his village. Kilik is excited, happy, and maybe nervous on the day of his first hunt. (Accept any appropriate answers.)

2. Kilik's father teaches him the important landmarks, trails, place names, and geography of the area. Kilik needs to know this information because one day he will hunt alone and he needs understand the land.

3. The village is built in a valley on a raised flat area overlooking the river. There are mountains surrounding the valley. The village was built in that area because there is water and good hunting and gathering areas nearby. (Accept any other appropriate answers.)

4. The Chumash people (and all native people) have a great respect and love for Mother Earth. They recognize that the land, plants, animals, and water are the resources they need to survive so they are careful with their environment. Food, clothing, tools, medicine, baskets, housing materials are made from natural resources. (Accept any additional appropriate answers.)

5. The double halos predict a drastic change in the lives of the Chumash people. Evidence from the story: A hunter tells Solomol that strange people wearing odd clothing and speaking an odd language who seem to have more powers than the Chumash leaders have been seen on the lands of the Chumash as well as to the south. These strange people are Spanish soldiers and priests who have come to take the land of the Chumash people.

Words to Know
(in order of appearance in the story)

Chumash word: haku: hello

talisman: an object that is believed to have magical power and will bring good luck to the person who wears it

nocking: to put the notch in the end of an arrow on the bowstring

carcass: the dead body of an animal

scan: to look carefully, especially in search of something

generation: people born and living at the same time

foothills: low hills at the base of a mountain or mountain range

makeshift: temporary

projectile: any object thrown into space by force

halo: a glowing light that circles something

Chapter 3 - The Strangers
Questions

1. How would you describe Solomol and Kilik's preparations to hunt? Compare and contrast the differences in their camouflage. What large animals are they hunting?

2. Explain what Solomol does after Kilik kills the deer.

3. What is your definition of courage? How does Solomon define courage to Kilik?

4. How do you imagine Kilik is feeling after his first successful hunt and his discussion with Solomol? Explain your answer.

5. What conclusions can you draw about the strange visitors who arrive in the village during Hutash? Who are the visitors? What language do they speak? How do the people of the village react to their first meeting?

Answers

1. Solomol and Kilik begin the day of the hunt in a traditional and respectful way; they say a prayer to Grandfather Sun.
   Solomol and Kilik camouflage themselves so they can move as close to their prey as possible without being noticed by the animal. Solomol wears a deerskin on his back and a dried deer head and antlers tied under his chin with cordage or a strip of leather. Kilik only wears a deerskin covering his back and shoulders. He isn't experienced enough to balance the weight of the deer head and antlers yet.
   Solomol and Kilik are hunting deer and antelope. (Inform students that California native people did not hunt buffalo. The buffalo are not indigenous to California.)

2. After Kilik's arrow kills the deer, Solomol does the following:
   - Showing respect for the deer, Solomol places his hand on the deer's head and says a prayer thanking the deer for the food he will provide to the people in the village.

- Solomol tells Kilik that he has crossed into manhood and is proud of him.
- Solomol gives Kilik the talisman necklace that he was given by his own father on his first hunt.
- Solomol tells Kilik that his skills may be one day needed for more than hunting. He might have to protect his family from enemies.

3. Answers will vary for individual courage definitions.
Solomon's definition of courage: "Courage comes from within you by joining your mind to your heart." When necessary, your courage will rise up to protect loved ones, even if you are afraid.

4. Individual student answers may vary. Possible responses:
Kilik is happy and proud of his accomplishments and pleased that his father is proud of him. He is excited to receive the talisman necklace; a sign of tradition being passed on to the next generation. Kilik is suddenly unsure of himself when his father explains that as a man, he will have responsibilities in addition to hunting.

5. The visitors who arrive in the village during Hutash are Spanish soldiers and priests sent to build outposts for Spain. They believe all indigenous people are inferior human beings and need to be educated and civilized in the European way. (Text) They speak Spanish and use an Indian translator to help them communicate with the Chumash and possibly to gain their trust. (Inference) To help put the natives at ease, the translator says that the visitors want to make life better for the Chumash. (Text) The visitors immediately try to show their power by using "fire sticks" (guns), unknown to the native people, to impress and frighten them. (Example from text: Soldier shoots the gourds and shocks everyone.) The visitors make it known that they have more "power" than the Indians (Interpreter says that fire-sticks are better than bows and arrows.). The visitors say they will share their knowledge with the Chumash people if they agree to visit their camp. (Example from text: Interpreter's statement, "Come share food. See more powers. Learn truth of their knowledge.") The visitors are using tricks and fear to convince the Indians in the village to visit the camp. (Conclusion)

The Chumash people are friendly, curious, cautious, confused, and afraid. They have many opinions about what the strangers' visit means. (Example from text: The Twelve leaders' debate.)

Words to Know (in order of appearance in the story)

shrine: a holy or sacred place

camouflage: a way of hiding people or objects by making them look like the natural background.

doe: a female deer

buck: a male deer

sacrifice: to give up something valuable to help another person

threshold: beginning something new

overcome: to succeed in dealing with a problem or difficulty

venison: meat from a deer

envious: wanting to have what someone else has

bounty: a variety and generous amount of food

indigenous: a person, plant, or animal native to an area

tongue: language

interpreter: someone who translates between languages

proclaim: to announce or declare officially or publicly

gourd: a fruit with a hard, outer shell that is used to make rattles for music and containers for food and water

dismay: worry, disappointment, upset

awe: a strong feeling of respect sometimes mixed with fear or surprise

debate: to discuss, argue, dispute

timid: shy, fearful, lacking confidence

Chapter 4 - Buzzard Food
Questions

1. How many people are chosen to travel to the strangers' camp and who makes the decision? What evidence can you find that shows the chief does not trust the strangers? Do you agree with his reasoning? Explain your answer.

2. Describe what Kilik and Tuhuy see when they arrive at the strangers' camp. In your opinion, how might the characters feel at first?

3. How would you describe the language problems Kilik and his family find in the camp? How does this problem help the priests and soldiers? What can you conclude about the native languages in California?

4. What evidence from the text justifies the conclusion that the native people already living in the camp when Kilik arrives are treated poorly?

5. What facts or ideas show that the behavior of the priests and soldiers do not change when Kilik and his family arrive? What is it that the people of the Place of the River Turtles do not realize at the end of the first day of their visit?

Answers

1. The chief of the Place of the River Turtles chooses about fifty people to travel to the strangers' camp. The chief chooses the best village protectors to make the journey. He tells the men to take their bows and arrows and to be ready to defend the people. This evidence shows that the chief does not trust the strangers. (Accept reasonable responses with supporting evidence for student opinion.)

2. When Kilik and Tuhuy arrive, they see:
   - oak trees that have been cut down (Acorn gathered from the oak trees are important food for the native people.)
   - cattle (Animals unknown to the native people.)
   - adobe buildings and adobe brick making (European style buildings)
   - native people looking sad and tired and guarded by soldiers

- strange food
- natives plowing the fields

The characters may feel overwhelmed, curious, confused, or afraid. Accept reasonable responses for student opinion.

3. Kilik and his family do not understand the language spoken by the priests and soldiers. They also do not understand the languages of the other native people living at the camp. This is an advantage to the priests and soldiers because the native people are unaware of what is being said around them. Since communication among the native people is difficult, they remain isolated. This helps the priests and soldiers control the native people.
Student conclusion: There are many diverse California native languages.

4. Evidence from the text that the native people already living in the camp are treated poorly:
   - native people are given poor quality food
   - native people appear skinny, tired, sad
   - native people spend the days doing hard work
   - native people are always guarded by soldiers

5. The priests and soldiers continue to try to convince the native people that they will learn new skills, their lives will improve, they (the priests) only want the best for the native people, and they will be paid for their work. When the native people appear to want to leave, the priests show them beads; a bribe to stay. Also, the soldiers surround the native people to keep them in the camp. The people of the Place of the River Turtles are unaware that when they entered the camp, they will be captive; unable to leave.

Words to Know (in order of appearance in the story)

prattle: to talk for a long time

stocky: sturdy, chunky

acorn: rounded nut from an oak tree

salmon: a large edible fish with red or pink flesh

buzzard: a large hawk-like bird of prey with broad wings and a rounded tail

intention: plan, purpose

Chapter 5 - What's Going On Here?
Questions

1. Why do you think the Chumash people are separated on their first night in the camp? What reason does the interpreter give? Do you believe him? Why or why not?

2. Can you explain what is happening when the soldier insists that Kilik and Tuhuy wear the garments?

3. What motivates the soldiers to remove the men's bows, arrows, and spears while they sleep? Why do you think Solomol and Salapay do not continue to protest? What is the priest's message that the translator gives the men?

4. The translator tells Kilik's group, "Today you be blessed to begin new life. Leave savage ways behind and receive a new name." Explain what happens next, Kilik's reaction, and the outcome. Do you agree with the actions of the priests and soldiers? Why or why not?

5. What do Kilik, Solomol, and Salapay finally realize on the second morning in camp?

Chapter 5
Answers

1. The Chumash people are separated on their first night in the camp to begin to break down the family groups. This gives the priests and soldiers control and prevents the native people from leaving if family members are in unknown locations in the camp. (Accept additional reasonable answers.)
   The interpreter tells the people that if they are separated, it will be easier to protect them and keep track of. ("Make sure all are where they belong.")
   Opinions on the interpreter's comment will vary.

2. The soldiers and priests have no respect or understanding of the Chumash culture or traditions. The soldier is insisting that Kilik and Tuhuy wear the garments because dressing in the European way is the beginning of changing how the natives live. The soldier knocks Kilik down to show his control over the boys and to instill fear so they won't fight back or object.

3. The soldiers remove the native men's bows, arrows, and spears while they sleep so that the men will be helpless; unable to fight or escape. Solomol and Salapay do not continue to protest because the soldiers are pointing their "fire-sticks" at the men's heads. The priest's message that the translator tells the men is: "Man-in-sky has delivered you to us. And here you and our people will stay." He informs the men that they will not leave the camp.

4. After the translator says, "Today you be blessed to begin new life. Leave savage ways behind and receive a new name." the priest begins to baptize and rename the native people in Kilik's village. The priest gives the native people Spanish names and baptizes them into a new religion. The people are required to be renamed and baptized; to become European. Kilik objects; he does not want a new name and does not want to join the camp community. However, the soldiers force the native people to undergo the process with force if necessary. The soldier makes an example out of Kilik by shooting his gun near Kilik's head, drawing everyone's attention, forcing him to comply. Then he pushes Kilik, who trips and falls. This renaming and baptizing procedure is a step toward taking away the Chumash culture, tradition, and individual identity.
   Accept appropriate student opinion responses.

5. In the morning, Kilik, Solomol, and Salapay finally realize that they will not be leaving the camp. They are not guests; they are captives.

Words to Know (in order of appearance in the story)

garment: an item of clothing

adequate: enough, suitable, satisfactory

gibberish: nonsense, meaningless speech

trudge: a long, slow, difficult walk

savage: people considered to be primitive and uncivilized

escort: to guide, lead

Chapter 6 - Coyote Men
Questions

1. What is the main idea of Chapter 6?

2. What is the "loud clanging sound" and what is its purpose? (Use clues from the story.) How are the "loud clanging sounds" and the strange food related to controlling the native people?

3. Describe the job Kilik and Tuhuy are given and its importance.

4. What advice does the translator give to Kilik and Tuhuy? What warning does he give them?

Chapter 6
Answers

1. The main idea of Chapter 6: Although the priests promise a new life, the priests and soldiers use force and brutality to make Chumash people of the Place of the River Turtles become slaves of the Spanish mission system.

2. The loud clanging sound is made by bells in the camp. The lives of the native people in the camp are regulated by the ringing of the bells; they must follow the schedule of the bells. The bells keep the people moving from task to task in a regimented way; lining up, waiting, working, eating, sleeping. This makes them easier to guard. The strange food keeps the native people hungry, poorly nourished, and tired. Tired, hungry people are less likely to fight the soldiers or try to escape.

3. Kilik and Tuhuy are assigned jobs making adobe bricks. (This job existed in all of the missions.) The bricks are used to make the European style buildings. The bricks are made by mixing water, dirt, and dried grass together. The mixture is placed into a wooden frame and dried in the sun. The brick is later removed from the frame. Kilik and Tuuy haul water from the river for brick making. It is hard work to make the bricks and a large supply is necessary for making the buildings of the new Mission.

4. Advice given to Kilik and Tuhuy by the translator:
    - Don't mention Chumash names in front of the priests; there will be punishment.
    - Keep busy and there won't be trouble.

   Warning given to Kilik and Tuhuy by the translator:
    - Don't try to run away, you will be captured, brought back, and punished.

   Words to Know (in order of appearance in the story)

usher: to show or guide someone somewhere

brisk: fast, quick

drone: to go on and on talking in a dull tone

adobe: a sun-dried brick made from a mixture of dirt, water, and dried grass

Chapter 7 - The Bells
Questions

1. In your opinion, what are four of the biggest adjustments the Chumash people are required to make in their daily lives?

2. The Chumash people did not dare contradict or question the padres directly. Do you agree with this decision? Why or why not?
   When did Kilik and his family have an opportunity to quietly break the rules? Why was this important?

3. List some of the jobs the native people must do at the mission. Do men and women work at the same jobs? What must both men and women do daily?

4. The padres' strict rules have punishments. Describe what the padres believe about the Indians and punishment. What offences are punished? What are the punishments?

5. Kilik, Solomol, and Salapay have specific concerns or worries. How would you describe and evaluate their concerns?

Answers

1. Four of the biggest adjustments the Chumash people are required to make:
   - Language; must learn Spanish, not allowed to speak native language
   - Religion; must learn Catholic religion
   - Separated from family members
   - Hard physical work
   - Insufficient food
   - Illness
   - Fear of punishment

   Accept any additional reasonable answers.

2. Student opinion replies will vary as to why the Chumash people did not dare to contradict or question the padres but should include fear of severe punishment and the human will to survive.

Chapter 7 Answers

3. Kilik and his family quietly break the rules at mealtime at the mission. This is important because it is an opportunity to speak their native language, remember who they are, where they come from, and to keep hope alive.

4. Men and women work at separate jobs in the mission.
   Men's jobs: brick making, building construction, field work, planting, harvesting, cattle/animal care, blacksmith work

   Women's jobs: laundry, weaving cloth, cooking, cleaning, working in vegetable gardens

   Men and women are required to study the Bible and learn to speak Spanish.

5. The padres think the Indians are children and they must have physical punishment when they break the rules. The padres believe this is the only way they will learn.
   Offenses: speaking native language, not working, meeting friends, escaping, contradicting the padres or soldiers
   Punishments: include whipping, stocks, hobbling feet, washing mouth with soap, hitting, pushing, capture

6. Solomol and Salapay are concerned that the others from their village will look for them and also become captive. They don't want anyone else from their village to be taken.

7. Kilik is worried about the changes he sees in his sister, Stuk's, behavior. She has changed from talkative, outgoing, and curious to withdrawn and quiet. (This is symbolic of the effect of the harsh treatment the Indians received at all of the missions; resulting in a loss of hope and spirit.)

Chapter 7
Words to Know (in order of appearance in the story)

padre: Spanish word for priest

contradict: challenge, argue against, deny

loom: a tool for weaving threads into cloth

stocks: feet and ankles are locked into the device and legs held out straight; used as a harsh punishment

hobble: to tie a strap around the feet to make walking difficult; used as a harsh punishment

Chapter 8 - The Secret Plan
Questions

1. Who are the "trustees"? What is their purpose? How do the padres motivate the trustees?

2. Why do Salapay and Solomol plan an escape? What is the result? How might it have ended differently?

3. The brutal punishment that Slomol and Salapay receive is a consequence of their escape plan. What other purpose does the punishment serve? Use evidence from the story to support your answer.

4. What judgment would you make about Father Espíritu? Support your comments with examples from the story.

5. What advantages do Kilik and Tuhuy have when they begin working as Father Espíritu's assistants? What important information do they learn?

Chapter 8 Answers

- The trustees are Indians who have been at the mission for a long time and speak Spanish well. The padres choose them. The trustees make sure the Indians are following the rules and report any problems or rule breaking to the padres and soldiers. If the trustee does not do his job, he and his family will be punished.

- Solomol and Salapay decide to plan an escape because they realize what a horrible place the mission is and they want to protect their families and people. The plan is ruined by a trustee, Reynaldo, who reports them. Answers for how the situation might have ended differently will vary.

- The flogging of Solomol and Slapay serves to physically hurt and punish the men for their escape plan. It also makes an example of them to the other native people; discouraging others from trying to escape. This breaks down the hope of the people and reinforces fear of the soldiers and trustees. By allowing the trustee to participate in the flogging, a separation and lack of trust develops between the native people.

- Opinions about Father Espíritu will vary but should be supported by examples from the text. Father Espíritu wants to covert the Indians but feels they should not be harshly punished. He is a much kinder man than Father Fiero. Examples from text:
    - Father Espíritu thinks Father Fiero treats the Indians too cruelly, he confronts Father Fiero and says he will write a complaint letter to the head of the Missions in Mexico City.
    - When Salapay and Solomol are flogged, Father Espíritu wants to give them medicine for their wounds, but Fiero won't let him.
    - Father Espíritu feels sorry for Kilik's and Tuhuy's fathers and offers them jobs as his assistants. He admits to them that he feels Father Fiero's punishments are too harsh.

- When Kilik and Tuhuy begin working for Father Espíritu, they no longer have to do the hard work of making adobe bricks or working in the fields in the hot sun. They also have the opportunity to overhear conversations between the priests and gather information to share with other native people in the mission. Kilik and Tuhuy learn that originally the native people would be released from the Mission when they became "civilized."

Chapter 8
Words to Know
(in order of appearance in the story)

trustee: a person who works for those in charge and makes sure rules are followed

incentive: something that encourages a person to do something

cohesive: when parts fit together, united

co-conspirators: people involved in a secret plan

flog: to beat someone with a whip or stick as a punishment or torture

mete: give out carefully

civilized: a high level of social, cultural, and technological development

Chapter 9 - A Small Vacation
Questions

1. What conclusions can you make about the effects of the flogging on the native people living at the mission?

2. Compare and contrast the motives of Father Espíritu, Father Fiero, and Captain Castigar regarding "the small vacation".

3. List two ways the soldiers were disrespectful to the Indians during the day away from the mission.

4. Explain the information the village elder tells Solomol and Salapay when the group visits their home, Place of the River Turtles.

5. What information does the visit to the village give you about the effect of the missions on native people left behind in the villages?

Chapter 9 Answers

1. The flogging upsets and depresses the other native people in the mission. They don't want to work as hard as they did before even when they are punished. They feel helpless, resentful, and probably hate the priests and soldiers more than before.
A consequence of the flogging for the priests is lower production of goods made at the mission. This results in less money earned for the mission.

2. Father Espíritu is sympathetic to the Indians. He feels sorry for them after the flogging and wants to raise their spirits.
Father Fiero wants the Indians to start working and producing again. He is convinced by Father Espíritu that the day away from the mission will help.
Captain Castigar wants to show the native people that their village is abandoned and they don't have homes to return to. This reinforces his control over the Indians and their feeling of helplessness.

3. The soldiers are disrespectful to the Indians on the day of their trip away from the mission in these ways:
    - The soldiers eat and gorge themselves on the gathered and cooked food prepared by the Indian women. The Indians must eat whatever is left.
    - Captain Castigar and the soldiers do not learn the Chumash language. Captain Castigar refers to the native language as "gibberish".
    - When the Chumash visit their village, Captain Castigar is "smug" and seems happy to see the village in ruins and abandoned.
    - The village elder they meet is left without food or help.

4. The village elder tells Solomol and Salapay that the Indians who have escaped from the missions are hiding at the base of Sacred Mountain.

5. The missions had an effect on all the native people, those taken captive and those left behind. People not taken to the mission were often the old ones. They were unable to provide for themselves left alone in the village. These people became sick, starved, and died. Those who escaped the missions had to stay in hiding so that they wouldn't be captured; they were not completely free.

Chapter 9
Words to Know (in order of appearance in the story)

witnessing: to see, watch, observe

escort: to lead

flee: to run away

snare: a type of woven trap

edible: safe to eat, can be eaten

skewer: a long piece of wood used for holding food together while cooking

gorge: eat greedily, fill up fast

eerily: strange, creepy

linger: to stay back

Chapter 10 - Is All Hope Lost?
Questions

1. Two years pass as captives in the mission for Kilik and his family. Summarize what this means for the priests and soldiers. Explain what it means for the native people. Use evidence from the story.

2. What conditions at the mission contribute to the high death rate among the native people? What statements in the chapter prove that the priests do not care about the Indians?

3. How would you describe the relationship between Kilik and Tuhuy after two years at the mission?

4. Discuss what some of the Chumash leaders do secretly and its importance.

5. At this point in the story, if you could speak to one of the native people living in the mission, what would you say?

Chapter 10 Answers

1. After two years, the mission's buildings are completed, crops, cattle, and products for sale and trade are being made. Indians are converted to the Catholic religion and are being "civilized". Even if by force, this all means success for the priests and soldiers. They are meeting their goals. For the Indians, the passage of time means a loss of physical and mental health, happiness, family, language, and culture. They are slaves living in the mission facing daily punishment. (Evidence from the text should be included.)

2. Conditions at the mission that contribute to the high death rate among the native people are: difficult and harsh working conditions, poor diets, severe physical punishment, untreated injuries, illness, and disease.

   Statements in the chapter that prove the priests' lack of concern for the native people:
   - "Most of those who died were unceremoniously placed in unmarked graves." (This occurred throughout the mission system.)
   - "…a padre marked down the name of the deceased and the date of his death in a big book, but that was all." (Record keeping)
   - "…these departed Indians were gone and forgotten by the Spaniards."

3. The relationship between Kilik and Tuhuy remains close and strong. Their shared difficult experiences have perhaps made their bond stronger. They continue to support and protect each other. They help each other stay positive and make games out of their work to avoid boredom. (Students may have additional comments and insights.)

4. The Chumash leaders continue to speak their language and mark traditional cycles of time the Chumash way. They are preserving the Chumash culture for future generations.

5. Student responses will vary.

Chapter 10 Words to Know

Advent: a period starting four Sundays before Christmas

Ash Wednesday: for Christians, first day of Lent, 46 days before Easter

Day of Ascension: Catholic celebration 40 days after Easter

Pentecost: a Christian feast on the seventh Sunday after Easter

coincided: to occur at the same time

Winter Solstice: shortest day of the year marking the beginning of winter

Summer Solstice: longest day of the year marking the beginning of summer

drudgery: hard or dull work

hoist: to raise something with ropes or pulleys

unceremoniously: informally, abruptly, rudely

Chapter 11 - News Spreads
Questions

1. What is the importance of the Spanish expedition?

2. Why do the priests and soldiers keep the news about the revolts at the other missions a secret?

3. What statement does Salapay make that illustrates the Indians are always being watched and are never safe?

4. Do you agree with Solomol's and Salapay's decision to lead a revolt? Explain your reasoning.

Chapter 11 Answers

1. The Spanish expedition brings supplies, mail, and news from other missions. The expedition leaves with hides, grains, and other items produced by the Indians for export.

2. The Spaniards keep the information about the revolts a secret because they don't want the Indians in their mission to decide to revolt as well. They don't want the Indians to think it's possible to revolt.

3. Salapay's statement: "Even the walls of the mission buildings seem to have ears."

4. Student opinions will vary.

Words to Know

expedition: a journey by a group of people with a specific purpose

export: to ship goods to another country for sale

revolt: to fight against the rule of a leader or government

rebellion: to rise up and fight those in power

squelch: to put an end to something such as an argument

embolden: to give courage or confidence

urgency: requiring immediate, quick action

quell: to put an end to something

allies: people or groups in agreement; working together toward a common goal

pledge: promise

Chapter 12 - The Countdown Begins
Questions

1. How do Indians pass messages between the missions? Why do you think the priests and soldiers are not aware of what the Indians are doing? What message is delivered to Solomol's group?

2. When will the attack happen? How long do the Indians have to prepare?

3. What does Solomol say his reason for fighting is? Do you think Solomol is confident that the revolt will be successful? Explain your answer.

4. What evidence shows that Father Espíritu knows a revolt is going to happen?

Answers

1. Messages are passed between the missions by the Indians who travel with the expeditions. The visiting Indians from the expeditions eat and sleep with the mission Indians and have opportunities to share information.

   Possible response: The priests and soldiers don't realize what the Indians are doing because they may underestimate the Indians' knowledge of what is happening, they think the Indians are ignorant and uninformed, they may think the soldiers are guarding the Indians well enough to keep them from communicating. (Student opinions will vary, statements should be supported with evidence from the story.)

   Solomol learns from the Indians in the expedition that native people who have escaped other missions and live nearby plan an attack on the mission.

2. The attack will occur on the Summer Solstice, in the early morning while the soldiers are eating breakfast. The Indians living in the mission have one week to prepare.

Chapter 12 Answers

3. Solomol's reason for fighting is to provide a successful escape for the children. He realizes that in order for the Chumash people to survive, the children must escape.
   Solomol is not confident that the revolt will be successful. He says, "IF the rebellion fails, the future of the Chumash people is the younger generation." He is also aware that the soldiers' weapons are more powerful that the Indians' bows and arrows. (Accept additional reasonable replies.)

4. Father Espíritu gives medical supplies and a burlap bag of "traveling food" to Kilik and Tuhuy. He also tells the boys that he doesn't approve of the treatment of the Indians at the mission.

Words to Know

quarters: shelter, house

overheard: to hear what other people are saying without them knowing

inspire: to make someone feel that they want to do something

agonize: to worry

capable: able to do something

chapel: a small church

burlap: a rough cloth made from jute or hemp and used mostly for bags

dorm (dormitory): a large room for sleeping

pine nuts: the edible seed of pine trees

chia seeds: seeds used as food from a native plant

Chapter 13 - Summer Solstice
Questions

1. Describe the events and mood in the mission on the morning of the Summer Solstice?

2. Why did Father Espíritu choose to help Kilik, Tuhuy, and the native children? What does he do? In your opinion, is Father Espíritu a brave man? Explain.

3. Imagine you are in the chapel with Kilik and Tuhuy and the native children, what would you be thinking and feeling?

Answers

1. Events on the morning of the Summer Solstice:
    - The Indians take weapons from storage room and hide them.
    - Attacking Indians charge the mission.
    - Children led by Kilik and Tuhuy run to safety in the chapel.
    - Reynaldo is sent to the Presidio for help for the soldiers.
    - The fighting begins between the soldiers and Indians.

    The mood in the mission that morning is tense, anxious, fearful, angry, and possibly hopeful. (Answers will vary. Accept reasonable replies.)

2. Father Espíritu unlocks the doors to the chapel so that Kilik, Tuhuy, and the children can go inside and be safe. He tells Kilik that he is helping because he doesn't agree with the Church's treatment of the Indians. He seems to care about the children.
    Father Espíritu risks being found out by the other priests and soldiers. He can be considered brave for putting the well-being of the native children over his own safety and reputation. (Opinions may vary.)
    (During the time of the missions, priests who openly objected to the treatment of the Indians were sent back to Mexico City or other locations.)

3. Accept reasonable, thoughtful replies.

Words to Know

nocturnal: active at night

stern: strict, serious

rendezvous: meet at agreed time and place

cot: a portable or folding bed

unison: at the same time, together

massive: large and heavy or solid

retreat: moving back or to withdraw

barricade: to block something so that people or things cannot enter or leave

presidio: a military post

sanctuary: a place of safety

Chapter 14 - A Near Miss
Questions

1. What role do Kilik and Tuhuy have in the revolt?

2. Can you predict what would have happened if Father Espíritu had not been waiting at the chapel with the keys to the door?

3. How do Kilik and Tuhuy continue to work together and use their special skills to keep the native children safe in the chapel?

4. If you could speak to Solomol and Salapay on the afternoon of the revolt, what would you tell them?

Chapter 14 Answers

1. Kilik and Tuhuy are in charge of taking the native children to the chapel and keeping them hidden and safe during the fighting.

2. Answers will vary.

3. Kilik uses his coordination and running skills to retrieve the burlap bag of food for the children. Tuhuy uses his problem-solving skills (thinking skills) to devise a lock for the chapel doors.

4. Accept reasonable answers.

Words to Know

retrieve: to get or bring

frantic: fear, anxiety

courtyard: an open space surrounded by walls or buildings

plaza: an open public space

eruption: an outburst or explosion

crossfire: gunfire from two or more directions passing through the same area

vertical: in an up-down position, upright, at right angles to the horizon

Chapter 15 - Call of Duty
Questions

1. What surprise exists in the chapel and how do you think it might be important to Kilik, Tuhuy, and the children?

2. What great responsibility do Kilik and Tuhuy accept? Why must they do this alone? Do you think they will be successful?

3. List the skills and character traits Kilik needs for a successful escape.

4. If Solomol and Salapay know about the trap door in the chapel and the secret door on the mission wall, why do you suppose they don't just take their own families and escape?

Answers

1. A trap door is in the floor of the chapel behind the altar. It leads down a passage and to a secret door in the mission wall. The trap door can be an escape route for the children.

2. Kilik and Tuhuy must escape with the group of native children and find their way to the village of runaway natives at the base of Sacred Mountain. The adults will stay at the mission and fight, causing a distraction while the children escape. All of the Indians trying to escape at once will be too obvious; a large group will move slowly and be too easy to track by the soldiers. Children escaping might not be noticed. Students' opinions on the success of the escape will vary.

3. Kilik must rely on his knowledge of the geography of the land and how to move or travel without being seen. (As when tracking animals.) He needs to use his knowledge of the four directions. Kilik must use his hunting skills, knowledge of plants, fire making, and shelter building to feed and protect the children. Kilik must also rely on his courage, determination, and sense of duty that his father said he would have when needed.

4. Opinions why Solomol and Salapay don't make use of the trap door for an escape for themselves and their families leaving the others behind will vary, but should include loyalty, honor, duty.

Chapter 15 Words to Know

altar: a raised platform in a church where ceremonies are performed

engulf: to completely surround or cover

hobbling: to walk in an awkward way usually due to injury

volley: a burst or outpouring of many things at once

dawn: the first appearance of light in the sky before sunrise

Chapter 16 - The Final Escape
Questions

1. After leaving the mission, what obstacles do Kilik, Tuhuy, and the native children encounter?

2. How is an understanding of nature related to a successful escape for Kilik's group?

3. Can you predict the outcome of the escape and journey of Kilik, Tuhuy, and the native children? What do you think will happen to the native people in the mission?

4. What makes the event in this story important in California history? Use information from the story and your unit of study to explain your answer.

Answers

1. After leaving the mission, the obstacles Kilik, Tuhuy, and the native children meet are: difficult, slow walking off the trails, rain, hunger, fear of capture by soldiers, fatigue, cold, and broken-down shelters for sleeping. (Accept other reasonable answers.)

2. An understanding of nature is essential to a successful escape for Kilik, Tuhuy, and the children. Kilik knows how to follow the animal trails for safety and how to use the tall grass to hide in. He recognizes landmarks such as Mother Oak to guide their way. Kilik uses the

sounds of the horses' hooves and the flock of birds as warnings to hide. He knows what resources to use to make fire and find food. He understands to find his direction to travel, he must go to a high point (Shrine Mountain).

3. Predictions and opinions of the outcome of the escape and what will happen to those left at the mission will vary. Encourage students to use previous knowledge about mission history to make reasonable predictions and to support opinions.

4. Opinions on the importance of the event in the story in California history will vary. Answers may include: Spanish land acquisition by force, coerced religious conversion, destruction of native culture and languages, drastic decrease in native populations, change in environment due to introduction of non-native plants and animals.

Words to Know

pews: long benches with a back used to sit on in churches

mourning doves: a bird; a dove with a long tail, gray-brown back, sad call

beacon: a light set up high to guide, warn, or signal

expose: uncovered, unprotected

flock (birds): group of birds

roosting: birds resting, sleeping

retreat: withdraw from enemy, moving back

dedication: committed to a task or purpose

contemplate: to think about

foretelling: to predict

gratitude: thankfulness

Lands of Our Ancestors – Book 1
Student Projects*

The following suggested projects and activities will extend the learning of early California history across the curriculum. Each project meets at least one of the fourth grade History-Social Science Content Standards in section 4.2:

"Students describe the social, political, cultural, and economic life and interactions among people of California from the pre-Columbian societies to the Spanish mission and Mexican rancho periods."

The projects are appropriate for individual students, partners, or small groups. Completed projects can be presented to the entire class for shared learning. All materials needed for the projects are basic classroom and school supplies. Laptops, notebooks, and the school library are resources the students will also need.

***PLEASE NOTE:**

Some of the Student Projects listed here are easily adaptable for use with other of the three Lands of our Ancestors novels. And likewise, some of the Student Projects suggested for the other two novels can be adapted for use with Book 1.

Projects and Activities

1. History Through Storytelling (Standard 4.2.1)

Storytelling is an important element of native culture. The stories carry a tribe's (and a family's) history, teach lessons about how people should behave, explain how things came to be in the world, and teach how to care for the land and animals.

Group Project: The students will choose a California Native American story that interests them.
- The students should identify the origin of the story; Chumash, Tongva, Yokuts, Ohlone, or other California tribe or tribal group.
- Each student should read the story and the group can discuss what information was learned from the story about the tribe.
- Individuals in the group can research basic facts about the tribe. The facts should include: territory, homes, language, foods, clothing, natural resources, mission influence.
- The students will organize the story into a Reader's Theater script that they will present to the class. Students can read their parts and minimal props are needed.
- Tribal facts from group research can be shared before the presentation.

Individual Project: The student may follow the same procedure but adapt the story to share in the oral tradition.

Materials: California Indian stories, reference books, laptops, notebooks, journals, index cards, pencils, pens, any props for the presentation

Suggested California Indian stories:
Coyote and the Grasshoppers: A Pomo Legend, Gloria Dominic
Fire Race: A Karuk Coyote Tale, retold by Jonathan London
Native Ways, California Indian Stories and Memories, Malcolm Margolin
A Story of Seven Sisters, A Tongva Pleides Legend, Pamela Marx
When the Animals Were People, Kay Sanger
Two Bear Cubs, A Miwok Legend, retold by Robert D. San Souci
The Beginning of the Chumash, retold by Monique Sonoquie
The Rainbow Bridge, Audrey Wood
The Sugar Bear Story, Mary J. Yee

2. Recording History (Standard 4.2.3)

Primary sources are important resources to use when researching the past. In this activity the student will imagine that he is living in the 1700's and has been sent on one of the Spanish expeditions to record the progress of the missions and the sights and sounds of California.

Individual Journal Project: The student will:
- write journal entries, using appropriate dates, describing what he sees, eats, how he travels, his impressions of the missions, and the people he meets.
- describe the relationships among the soldiers, missionaries, and Indians.
- include drawings of native plants, animals, and other new natural resources that would be seen.
- use previous knowledge and new research to complete the project.

Materials: Journals, pencils, pens, colored pencils, laptops, resource books

3. Group Timeline Project: The students will:
- create a timeline from pre-mission to post-mission periods.
- use resources to research important facts and dates to post on the timeline.
- use drawings, photos, or other pictures to illustrate the timeline.
- display the timeline in the classroom.

Materials: Butcher paper, colored pencils, pens, paints, laptops, resource books

4. The Land (Standard 4.2.4)

The respect that the native people in Lands of Our Ancestors have for the land includes knowledge of the geography of their territory.

Group or Individual Project: The student will use the information from the story to draw a map of where the Chumash people from the Place of River Turtles built their village and the surrounding area. The map should include:
- the village
- the mission
- Sacred Mountain
- Shrine Mountain

- Mother Oak
- hunting area
- old camp
- animal trails
- river
- Pacific Ocean
- foothills
- the village where the runaway natives live
- nearby missions

Materials: Large construction paper or butcher paper, pens, colored pencils, paints, copy of story

5. Fact Box (Standard 4.2.5)

Group or Individual Project: This game activity reinforces new material learned in the unit of study and will motivate students to research additional information.

The student will cover and decorate a shoe box or similar size box. Decorations should illustrate one of the story themes or scenes. There should be an opening at the top of the box large enough to reach inside. Using index cards, the student will write 20 or more question cards about daily life in the missions for native and non-native people. Answers to the questions should be written on the back of the question cards. Questions can be true or false.
Examples:
Q: Who made the adobe bricks for the mission buildings?
A: The native men and boys made the adobe bricks.

Q: True or False? Native families were allowed to stay together and speak their native languages in the missions.
A: False

Students can play the game individually or in teams, taking turns choosing cards from the box. Students can decide if they want to keep score; awarding points for correct answers.

Materials: Shoe box, paper, scissors, tape, pencils, pens, crayons, index cards, laptop, resource books, copy of story

6. Compare and Contrast (Standard 4.2.5)

Group or Individual Project: Students will make three posters to be displayed side by side. Each poster will represent a different group; natives, priests, and soldiers living at the mission. Students will use words and pictures to illustrate each group's daily life. The side by side display will illustrate the contrast. This project can include an oral presentation or explanation of the information in the posters and students' opinions.

Materials: Poster board, pens, pencils, drawings or pictures, glue, laptop, resource books, copy of story

7. Native Plants (Standard 4.2.6)

Native people have always had great knowledge of plants; an important natural resource. Plants are used for food, medicine, and a variety of items ranging from cordage to sleeping mats to houses. Today, in modern times, native plants are being grown in yards and public spaces because they are drought tolerant. Native plants are also currently studied for their value in modern medicine.

Group or Individual Project: The student will choose at least four native plants used by Indians in California. The student will research the importance of the plants to the native people, the uses of the plants, where the plants grow, and any other interesting or important information. The student will research how the native plants are used today. (See plant list below.)
The student will assemble the information in a booklet or poster. Pictures of the plants should be included. The completed project can be shared with the class and displayed. Alternate display: collage of plants and information.

If space allows, students can plan and plant a native garden on school grounds or in planters.

Materials: paper, journals, poster board, pens, pencils, crayons, laptops, native plant resource books, plant pictures

8. Native Plant Concentration Game (Standard 4.2.6)

Group or Individual Project: Student will write the names of at least ten native plant names on index cards of one color. Then the student will write the uses of the ten native plants on index cards of a different color. Cards can be decorated. To play the game: Shuffle the cards in both groups and match the name of the card with the use. Students can play in pairs. Students may invent other versions of the game.

Suggested native plants: willow, juncus, oak, elderberry, deergrass, yucca, agave, tule reeds, sage, milkweed, sumac, yerba mansa, soap root, manzanita, toyon.

Materials: colored index cards, pencils, crayons, native plant resource books, laptop

Lands of our Ancestors - Book Two Teacher's Guide

Developed by Dessa Drake
and Gary Robinson

Lands of Our Ancestors Book Two
Teacher's Guide Introduction

This Teacher's Guide is designed to enrich teaching Lands of Our Ancestors Book Two across the curriculum. The guide begins with the California Content Standards for 4th grade History-Social Sciences the book addresses. This information will provide the teacher with important information about what the focus should be in teaching the Mexican Rancho Unit. This is followed by an Overview of the Mexican Rancho period in California history. In addition, there are pages of images of life during the Rancho Era. These images help illustrate the story. At this point the guide also includes a section that validates the accuracy of the events portrayed in the story and a list of sources of further information on the Chumash people and the historic ranchos and adobes.

The eighth section of the guide contains the same "Characters and Relationships" reference as well as the "Timeline" found in the book. Section ten, the largest section of this guide, contains "Questions, Answers, and Words to Know" for each chapter of Book Two. The questions can be used in teacher-directed class discussions, small group discussions, or as written work. The variety of questions in each chapter align with The Six Levels of Questioning: knowledge, comprehension, application, analysis, synthesis, evaluation. Answers are provided for all chapter questions. New vocabulary, including words from the Samala Chumash, Yokuts, and Spanish languages, are found in each chapter's "Words to Know" page.

Finally, to extend the learning after the book is completed, the guide includes possible project choices to engage students. The projects are designed to meet the needs of the diverse learners found in most classrooms. Each project meets a specific fourth grade History-Social Science Content Standard for California Public Schools. The standard is listed with each project.

Students who complete reading the story, discuss or write responses to the questions, and learn the new vocabulary words will meet a variety of the fourth grade California Common Core State Standards in reading, writing, and language.

California Fourth Grade History Social-Science Standards

4.2 Students describe the social, political, cultural, and economic life and interactions among people of California from the pre-Columbian societies to the Spanish mission and Mexican rancho periods.

> 4.2.5: Describe the daily lives of the people, native and nonnative, who occupied the presidios, missions, ranchos, and pueblos.
>
> 4.2.6: Discuss the role of the Franciscans in changing the economy of California from a hunter-gatherer economy to an agricultural economy.
>
> 4.2.7: Describe the effects of the Mexican War for Independence on Alta California, including its effects on the territorial boundaries of North America.
>
> 4.2.8: Discuss the period of Mexican rule in California and its attributes, including land grants, secularization of the missions, and the rise of the rancho economy.

from *https://www.cde.ca.gov/be/st/ss/documents/histsocscistnd.pdf*

We recommend also consulting the California History Social Studies Framework for additional background information. The framework focuses on missions and the rancho period beginning on page 9 of the PDF version found at https://www.cde.ca.gov/ci/hs/cf/documents/hssfwchapter7.pdf

Overview of the Mexican Rancho Period

Mexico achieved independence from Spain in 1821 and created a functioning republic in 1824. During this time, and for several decades afterwards, the new nation suffered through periods of strife between competing factions vying for very different forms of government. In Mexican California, this instability deeply affected the Indian population at the missions, contributing to the decline of the missions. It was during this time that the most serious mission uprisings occurred.

Contributing to the decline of the missions were the thousands of neophytes who simply fled when conditions became intolerable, as well as the thousands of Indians who died from disease. In 1821, the number of neophytes at the various missions peaked at 21,000, but by 1834, less than 16,000 remained.

In 1833, the Mexican government passed a law that secularized the missions. The law required the missions to give up control over the neophytes and the missions were to be converted into pueblos with lands distributed among the Indians living there. Livestock, equipment and seeds previously belonging to the missions were also supposed to be supplied to the freed neophytes.

However, most of the land and property designated for the ex-neophytes fell into the hands of the Californios and were turned into private estates called ranchos. Many of the Indians were driven off. Some drifted into Mexican towns looking for jobs, while others found work on the ranchos. Still others moved to the interior regions of California hoping to find relatives or fellow tribesmen already living there.

By the mid-1830s, the ranchos were growing and the demand for cheap labor increased. It was the ex-neophytes who flocked to the pueblos and ranchos who filled this demand. Away from the towns, the vast majority of Indians worked for the Californios on ranchos. Although the ranchos were organized to sell products and turn a profit, in reality they produced little marketable goods. Instead, they were basically subsistence institutions, producing only enough to support their Mexican and Indian residents.

Unlike the missions, where all aspects of the lives of the neophytes were strictly regulated, the rancheros were not concerned with the non-economic activities of their Indian workers. Some rancheros allowed families and kin groups to remain intact and community life to continue relatively undisturbed. Even so, the rancheros relegated their Indian workers to a dependency position because the Indians were paid "in kind" and not in cash. The land upon which they built their villages and raised their crops and animals were controlled by the rancheros.

California Indians were economically important to the successful operation of the ranchos as reflected in a statement made by a prominent ranchero:

Many of the rich men of the country had from twenty to sixty Indian servants whom they dressed and fed.... Indians tilled our soil, pastured our cattle, sheared our sheep, cut our lumber, built our houses, paddled our boats, made tiles for our homes, ground our grain, slaughtered our cattle, dressed their hides for market, and made our unburnt bricks; while the Indian women made excellent servants, took good care of our children, made very one of our meals...

-Salvador Vallejo in Cook 1943b:51

Independent Indians from the interior frequently raided coastal ranchos, not to destroy lives or property, but to capture horses. The enormous herds of horses were easy and tempting targets, and the Indians preferred them to cattle as a food source because they were easier to drive off. The animals also fulfilled transportation and trade needs. Indians continually raided the ranchos' horse herds, and this continued well into the 1870s, long after the Americans took over California. By substituting new food sources for those wiped out by Spanish and Mexican settlements, many Indians became heavy consumers of meat. This dietary change saved entire villages from starvation.

As Mexican settlements expanded, the Mexican military, responding to the demands for new laborers, began raiding interior Indian groups for laborers; thus Native resistance began to stiffen. Formerly peaceful, sedentary, localized groups changed to semi-warlike, semi-nomadic groups and began to take the offensive. Adopting guerilla warfare tactics, interior people underwent considerable physical and military adaptation. In the central valley, the Indian offensive reached a peak in 1845; in fact, so successful were Indian raids on coastal settlements that the Mexican government resolved to establish a military border police and erect a fort at Pacheco Pass to prevent further raids.

Mexican authorities and land barons also responded to such raids with punitive expeditions against the interior people, resulting in enslavement of many Indians and acts against them of almost unheard of barbarity. For example, in 1837, José Marí Amador, a wealthy rancher, led a party of civilians, soldiers, and Indian auxiliaries on an expedition into the San Joaquin Valley, where they encountered a group of about 200 suspected wrongdoers, including 100 or so ex-neophytes. Amador wrote that he *"invited the wild Indians and their Christian companions to come and have a feast."* When the Indians came into the Mexican's camp, armed members of the expedition who had been in hiding surrounded the Indians and quickly subdued them. Amador then separated out the Christian Indians and, as he wrote,

At every half-mile or mile, we put six of them on their knees, making them understand that they were about to die. Each one was shot with four arrows, two in front and two in the back. Those who refused to die immediately were killed with spears. On the road were killed in this manner the 100 Christians.

Later Amador decided to execute the unconverted prisoners, after he first baptized them.

I ordered Nazario Galindo to take a bottle of water and I took another. He began at one part of the crowd and I at another. We baptized all the Indians and afterwards they were shot in the back. At the first volley, 70 fell dead. I doubled the charge for the 30 who remained, and they all fell.

Even more devastating to Indians in the Central Valley than such murderous expeditions were the whites' diseases. In the early 1830s, trappers for the Hudson's Bay Company passed through the Great Valley, introducing malaria into the marshy interior lowlands. The disease killed an estimated 20,000 Indians and remained endemic thereafter. By the end of the Mexican occupation, the total Native population of California had been reduced to about 100,000 persons.

Images of Mexican Rancho Life

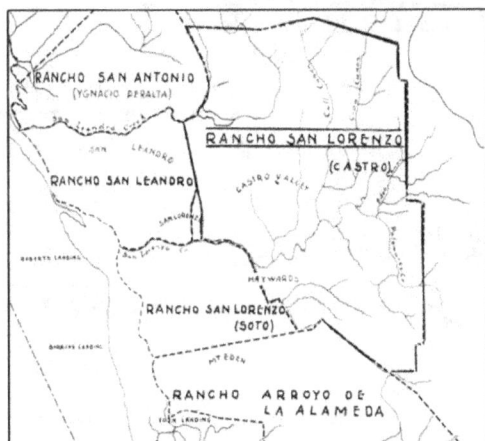

ABOVE: Example of a two story Mexican Rancho house similar to the one described in <u>Lands of our Ancestors Book Two</u>.
-*Petaluma Adobe State Historic Park*

LEFT: Example of Mexican Rancho map that shows the boundary lines of neighboring ranchos. This map shows ranchos in Alameda County near Hayward.
-*Hayward Area Historical Society*

RIGHT: Example of work space and storage area inside the first floor of a rancho house like the one described in <u>Lands of our Ancestors Book Two</u>.

Images of Mexican Rancho Life - Page 2

LEFT: Vaquero at work on a Mexican Rancho around 1830. - *Artist unknown. Image in public domain.*

RIGHT: Examples of Mexican Rancho cattle brands similar to the one described in Lands of our Ancestors Book Two.

Rancheros and their Brands

Francisco Badillo	Luis Arellanes	Juan Rodriguez
José de la Guerra	Patricio Cota	Antonio Ruiz
Octaviano Gutierrez	Narciso Fabrigat	José Lugo
Juan Camarillo	Juan Cordero	Juan Pico
Refugio Carrillo	José Ortega	Rita Ontiveros
Santa Barbara Mission	Augustin Janssens	Maria Sanchez

LEFT: Example of a bull and bear fight similar to the one described in Lands of our Ancestors Book Two. These were common forms of entertainment for people of the Mexican Ranchos. -*"Sport in California, A Bull and Bear Fight" by Samuel Waller; Look and Learn/ Bridgeman Images*

Examples of Traditional California Native Structures

Chumash House - Ap (op)

Styles of Yokuts Houses

One Example of Native Sweat House showing underground cutaway. Other similar designs were used by California tribes.

Accuracy of Events Portrayed in Lands of our Ancestors Book Two

This work of historical fiction depicts what <u>might</u> have happened to California Native Americans as Alta California transitioned from Spanish control to Mexican control in the 1820s to 1830s. Although the characters and the specific plot are fictional, the people and events in the book are based on, and taken from, historical documents and the historical writings of non-fiction authors and scholars.

More specifically, for example, many of the details of California rancho life for Native Americans came directly from Stephen W. Silliman's <u>Lost Laborers in Colonial California: Native Americans and the Archaeology of Rancho Petaluma</u>. Silliman's work at Petaluma reveals much about daily life, ranch organization, living and labor conditions, living quarters and annual activities at a California Mexican rancho.

Scenes depicting activities of the vaqueros can be found in multiple historical print and image sources, as can descriptions of the bull and bear fight, which served as entertainment for the regular amusement of the region's Californios.

The battle scenes between Indians and Mexican soldiers depicted in Chapters 12 and 13 of <u>Lands of our Ancestors Book Two</u> are derived from the last three chapters of Elias Castillo's exhaustively researched <u>A Cross of Thorns</u>. That work, in turn, relied on earlier historical works, particularly the anthology <u>Native American Perspectives on the Hispanic Colonization of Alta California</u>, published in 1991, edited by California Native author Edward D. Castillo.

However, in many cases, the way Native Americans were treated during the Mexican Rancho period depended on the nature and beliefs of the *rancheros* (ranch owners) themselves. A few Native *rancho* laborers enjoyed more freedoms and better conditions than those depicted in the Lands of our Ancestors series.

However the period is depicted, the truth is that the Mexican Rancho period contributed heavily to the further destruction and devastation of Native American peoples, communities and cultures in the region that became known as California.

Sources on the Chumash People:

1. California's Chumash Indians, A Project of the Santa Barbara Museum of Natural History; EZ Nature Books; 1992, Revised Edition 2002.
2. The Chumash, Seafarers of the Pacific Coast; Karen Bush Gibson; Capstone Press, 2004.
3. "The Samala People" (DVD); produced by the Santa Ynez Band of Chumash Indians; Available from the tribe's Culture Department; 805-688-7997.
4. Bad Indians: A Tribal Memoir; Deborah A. Miranda; Heyday, 2013.
5. Samala-English Dictionary-A Guide to the Samala Language of the Ineseno Chumash People; Santa Ynez Band of Chumash Indians with Richard Applegate, PhD; 2007.
6. Website: www.sbnature.org/research/anthro/chumash/intro.htm (Chumash section of the Santa Barbara Museum of Natural History's website)
7. Website: www.santaynezchumash.org/history.html (The Santa Ynez Band of Chumash Indians official website)
8. Wikipedia Website: https://en.wikipedia.org/wiki/Chumash_people.

Sources on Mexican Ranchos in California:

1. Silliman, Stephen W. Lost Laborers in Colonial California: Native Americans and the Archaeology of Rancho Petaluma. University of Arizona Press, Tucson, 2004.
2. Castillo, Elias. Cross of Thorns: The Enslavement of California's Indians by the Spanish Missions. Craven Street Books, Fresno, 2015.

3. Timbrook, Jan. <u>Chumash Ethnobotany: Plant Knowledge Among the Chumash People of Southern California</u>. Santa Barbara Museum of Nat'l History, Santa Barbara, 2007.

4. Richard Applegate and the Santa Ynez Chumash Education Committee. <u>Samala-English Dictionary: A Guide to the Samala Language of the Ineseño Chumash People</u>. 2007.

5. John P. Harrington's field notes from Maria Solares, Fernando Librado and other Native California consultants. Available through the J.P. Harrington Database Project located in the Culture Department of the Pechanga Tribe near Temecula, California.

6. Cook, Sherburne F. <u>The Conflict Between the California Indian and White Civilization</u>. University of California Press, 1976.

Characters and Relationships in the <u>Lands of our Ancestors</u> series

Kilik (Miguel) – main character, son of Solomol and Wonono

Tuhuy (Rafael) – Kilik's cousin, son of Salapay and Yol

Stuk (Maria) – Kilik's younger sister

Solomol – Kilik's father

Salapay – Tuhuy's father

Wonono – Kilik's mother

Yol – Tuhuy's mother

Alol-koy – Chumash boy with the children who escaped the mission

Tah-chi – Yokuts Indian scout for the Place of Condors village

Lau-lau – Kilik's first wife

Kai-ina – Kilik's second wife, mother of Malik

Toh-yosh – Lead warrior for the Place of Condors village

Taya – Tuhuy's Chumash wife

Alapay (Andrea) – Tuhuy's daughter and Malik's cousin

Malik (Mateo) – Kilik's son and Andrea's cousin

Mo-Loke – Chumash elder in the Place of Condors village

Diego – Native outlaw and leader of Indians who attacked ranches

Francisco Pacheco – Mexican Ranch owner of *Rancho Caballeros*

Mrs. Pacheco – Ranch owner's wife, mother of Magdalena

Magdalena – Ranch owner's daughter

Esteban - Ranch foreman at *Rancho Caballero*

Pedro – Assistant foreman at *Rancho Caballero*

Timeline of Historical and Fictional Events in the Lands of our Ancestors series

1769	First Spanish mission established near what is now San Diego
1776	Solomol is born at the Place of River Turtles village
1777	Salapay is born at the Place of River Turtles village
1792	Kilik is born (when Solomol is 16)
1793	Tuhuy is born
1797	Kilik's sister Stuk is born
1804	Kilik & family go to the new mission
1806	The children escape the mission on Summer Solstice morning
	The children arrive at the Place of Condors village
1811	Kilik marries Lau-lau (Yokuts) - Kilik is 19
1812	Dec. 21 - Earthquake damages missions in Chumash territory
	Kilik's unborn baby and wife die the day of the earthquake
1813	Stuk dies from measles brought to the village by visitor
1814	Tuhuy leaves village to live alone, study healing, contact ancestors
	Kilik leaves village to explore the region and to raid missions and ranches
1819	Kilik returns to village, meets Kai-ina (Yokuts woman)
	Tuhuy returns to village, sees Taya (Coastal Chumash)
1820	Tuhuy marries Taya - Tuhuy is 27
	Simultaneous wedding ceremony: Kilik marries Kai-ina
1821	Malik is born to Kilik (who is 29 years old) & Kai-ina
	Mexico wins independence from Spain
1822	Alapay is born to Tuhuy and Taya
1823+	Cousins Malik and Alapay grow and play together
1824	Kilik begins raiding ranches and missions for cattle - age 32

1825-30	Alapay blends healing and fighting as needed
1832	Kilik turns 40 years old
1833	Tuhuy turns 40 years old
1833	Kilik trains Malik as hunter & warrior
	Alapay learns hunting and fighting skills as well
	Spanish padres expelled from missions - Mission Indians released
	Francisco Pacheco gets major land grant - needs laborers
	Epidemic outbreak (flu or malaria)
1834-1848	Major Mexican *Rancho* Period
1834	Kilik finds crippled father, brings him and aunt Yol back
	Pacheco's men raid Condor Village; take Tuhuy and others to *Rancho Caballeros*
	Tuhuy and everyone held at ranch, must work
	Kilik raids Rancho Caballero, rescues family

74

Chapter Questions & Answers

Words to Know

Chapter 1 - Survival Skills
Questions

1. Describe the main characters Kilik and Tuhuy. In what ways are they the same characters from Book One?

2. Summarize this chapter. What exactly are Kilik and Tuhuy doing and why?

3. List some steps the children take to keep from getting caught.

4. Based on what occurs in this chapter, do you think Salapay and Solomol were right to place such a responsibility on their young sons? Cite evidence to explain your reasoning.

Answers

1. Kilik is 14 years old. He is still very much a leader. He is skilled at hunting.

   Tuhuy is 13 years old. He is still very much a thinker. He remembers the words of his elders.

   The boys still work together well.

2. Kilik and Tuhuy are in the midst of an escape from the mission. Although Kilik was put in charge by his father, both boys are trying to help a small group of children reach Sacred Mountain and hopefully, freedom.

3. They choose a hidden spot near a creek to camp, they stay off of the main trails, and they are aware of whether or not it is safe to build a fire.

4. Answers may vary, but evidence cited might include: Alol-koy trusts the two as leaders; the boys have successfully brought the children this far, keeping them off the trails and providing them with food.

Chapter 1 Words to Know

<u>Chumash Names and Words</u>:

Kilik (K<u>ee</u>-leek): Sparrow Hawk; teenage boy
Tuhuy (Too-<u>hooy)</u>: Rain; teenage boy, Kilik's cousin
Stuk (Rhymes with Luke): Ladybug; Kilik's sister
Alol-koy: Dolphin; boy with the children who escaped the mission

Words to Know (in order of appearance in the story)

elder: a respectful term for those older than you in a tribe

shackles: U-shaped fastening devices secured by bolts that confine the legs or arms

Summer Solstice: the longest day of the year, when Grandfather Sun's power is strongest

quiver: a case for holding arrows, usually made from animal skin

Chapter 2 - The Village that Ran Away
Questions

1. What evidence from this chapter supports what we already know about the personalities of Kilik and Tuhuy?

2. Describe the Place of Condors. Why is it not like a typical Native village?

3. In this chapter, there is some foreshadowing about the futures of Kilik and Tuhuy, two boys who share a strong bond and whose paths have thus far been closely linked. What does it appear may lie ahead for these two cousins?

Chapter 2 Answers

1. Kilik, as a leader and boy of action, pokes around the abandoned village. He is eager to get the children safely to the new village. He takes to riding and working with the horses well.

   Tuhuy, the thinker, comforts the children. He wants to offer prayers up on Sacred Mountain. He increases his knowledge by learning how to plant crops and grow food.

2. The village has different housing: traditional Chumash dwellings and traditional Yokut dwellings. There is also a ceremonial area, playing field, and granary. Crops are being grown. Horses are corralled there. This is not a village of one tribe; it is a village of people from several tribes, survivors of the missions. They do not speak the same traditional languages or ways of living, but their experiences with the Spanish are the same. They are combining all of this in order to survive in this land that is not the same as it was before the Spanish arrived.

3. Tuhuy mentions a couple of times that he and his cousin may begin leading different paths. Kilik appears to be following the path of the warrior, whereas Tuhuy has been noticed by the elders as one who may become a healer and spiritual leader.

Chapter 2 Words to Know

<u>Yokuts Names:</u>

Tah-chi: Yokut scout given the name of his tribe as a nickname; guides the children to the Place of Condors

Toh-yosh: Arrow; leads the warriors of the Place of Condors

Words to Know (in order of appearance in the story)

approached: came nearer to

tule reeds: tall, green reeds with spongy stems

uprising: an act of resistance or rebellion; a revolt

emerge: to become known or apparent

Chapter 3 - Starting Over
Questions

1. When Kilik is sixteen and ventures out alone to search for his parents, an unexpected event occurs. What does this event demonstrate about him?

2. Kilik and Tuhuy's separate paths further develop in this chapter. Using a graphic organizer, map out the sequence of events for each character.

3. Do you agree with the way Kilik decided to deal with the loss of his wife, unborn child, and sister? Explain your reasoning.

Answers

1. Kilik is brave, but sometimes acts without thinking things through. He is smart, however; he did not lead the soldiers to the Place of Condors. His bravery and skill are tested and proven. He does not yet have the capability to kill another human being.

2. Kilik:

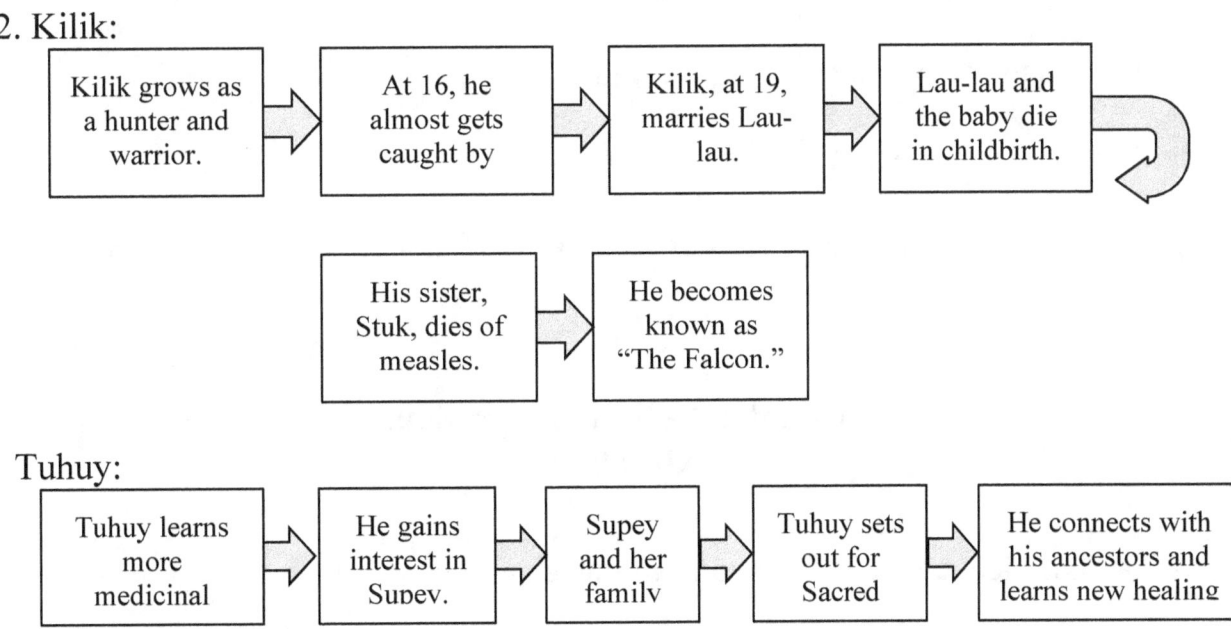

Tuhuy:

| Tuhuy learns more medicinal | → | He gains interest in Supey. | → | Supey and her family | → | Tuhuy sets out for Sacred | → | He connects with his ancestors and learns new healing |

3. Student answers will vary.

Chapter 3
Words to Know

<u>Yokuts Name:</u>

Lau-lau: Butterfly; Kilik's wife

<u>Samala Chumash Name:</u>

Supey: Ornament or adornment; Tuhuy's love interest

Words to Know (in order of appearance in the story)

malnutrition: lack of proper nutrition, caused by not having enough to eat, not eating enough of the right things, or being unable to use the food that one does eat

commandant: an officer in charge of a particular unit

hobbled: tied or strapped together to prevent escape

Winter Solstice: the shortest day of the year

honed: refined or perfected

notoriety: the state of being famous or well known for some bad quality or deed

Chapter 4 - New Generations
Questions

1. What historical event is referred to in this chapter?

2. Other events occur that affect or have the potential to affect Native people in California in this chapter. What are they?

3. Why do Kilik and Tuhuy give their children Spanish names? Why were they hesitant to do so?

Chapter 4 Answers

1. Mexico gains independence from Spain in 1821 and thus, control over Alta California.

2. Spanish colonizers are building towns and ranches throughout California. The traditional plants and herbs gathered by Native people are disappearing, as are the animals they would traditionally hunt. There is a drought.

3. Kilik and Tuhuy give their children Spanish names in case of future interactions with Californios or Mexican authorities, and also to protect them from those who might do them harm. The men are hesitant to give their children Spanish names because they want to maintain their Chumash traditions, not carry on a practice of the Spanish invaders.

Chapter 4 Words to Know

Yokuts Names and Words:

Kai-ina: Kilik's second wife - Yokuts

Chumash Names:

Taya: Abalone; Tuhuy's Chumash wife

Malik: First-Born Child; Kilik's son

Koko: Samala for "father"

Alapay: Above; Tuhuy's daughter

Chapter 4 Words to Know (in order of appearance in the story)

reunited: came together again after a period of separation

remote: far from the main centers of population

reluctantly: in an unwilling and hesitant way

cautious: careful to avoid potential problems or dangers

persevered: continued on despite facing difficulties or little chance of success

tumultuous: confusing, disorderly

Chapter 5 - More of the Same
Questions

1. Describe how each of the three historical events taking place in this chapter affected the Native people of California.

2. Contrast the European perspective of land with that of Native people. Which do you think is better, and why?

3. What details about a *rancho* do you learn from this chapter?

4. The characters in this book suffer repeated loss and tragedy, the knowledge of which is evident particularly in this chapter. What feelings would you have experienced if you were Kilik, upon learning of these additional losses? If you were Solomol? What do you think motivates them to keep going despite all of these hardships?

Chapter 5 Answers

1. The flu epidemic of 1833 caused thousands of deaths among Native people because they had no immunity or traditional medicines prepared to deal with this illness that came from Europeans.

   The closing of the missions in 1833 was supposed to return land to Native people, but few received any. Most had no home and no way to sustain themselves once the missions closed.

   The creation of large *ranchos* from the giving away of land grants created the need for a labor force. *Rancheros* like Francisco Pacheco used former mission Indians to fulfill this need.

2. Europeans believed in land ownership and divided up land for this purpose. This concept did not exist in Native California. Native people traditionally believed the land was given by Creator for all people. Opinions will vary, but should include reasoning.

3. *Ranchos* developed as a result of land grants being given to Californios by the Mexican government. Hundreds of them were given away. These land grants included thousands of acres of land, primarily for the purpose of raising cattle. Native people, mostly those that once lived and worked within the mission system, served as the labor force on the ranchos. Some of these Native laborers came willingly because they had nowhere else to go, but others were captured, much as they were during the mission period.

4. Answers will vary, but feelings may include grief, despair, anger, shock, sadness, loss of hope, a desire for revenge. Sources of motivation may be the love they have for their family, the survival of the tribe, the desire to see their children or grandchildren grow up, the desire to return to their homeland, or the refusal to allow the invaders to change their lifeways.

Chapter 5
Words to Know

Chumash Words:

'Unu: grandson

Mo-loke: ancient/long ago; elder left behind at the Place of Condors

Words to Know (in order of appearance in the story)

epidemic: a widespread occurrence of an infectious disease in a community at a particular time

ailment: a minor illness

expelled: forced to leave a place

land grant: a piece of land given by the Mexican government to Mexican citizens

abandoned: deserted

rancho: a cattle ranch

rations: a fixed amount of a commodity, such as food

vaqueros: cowboys; horse-mounted ranch hands

capable: able

vaguely: in a way that is uncertain or unclear

familiar: well known or recognizable

smoldering: burning slowly with smoke, but no flame

Chapter 6 - Kidnapped
Questions

1. Compare and contrast mission life and *rancho* life for Native laborers, using this chapter (and previous chapters) and your own prior knowledge.

2. Do you think Tuhuy's action at *Rancho Caballero* was wise? Why or why not?

3. If you were among those in this kidnapped group, how would you be feeling as you arrive at this rancho and observe and listen to what's in store for you?

Chapter 6 Answers

1. Like the missions, many of the buildings on a *rancho* were made of adobe bricks. Also, Native people did much/all of the labor. They received food, clothing, and a place to sleep in exchange for their labor. The main house of a rancho, like a mission, was typically built in the quadrangle formation, with a central courtyard. Indian servants tended to the needs of the *ranchero's* family much as they would the padres of a mission. Similar to the missions, Indian laborers produced several products on *ranchos*, including saddles, boots, rugs, candles, and blankets.

   Unlike the missions, families were not separated from each other on the *ranchos*. The focus of the *rancho* was cattle, so *vaqueros* were workers on ranchos that were not at the missions. This required many horses on a *rancho*, which was not necessary at a mission. A *rancho* included a main house that had two levels. The *ranchero* owned a *rancho*, whereas a mission was owned by the Spanish government and run by Spanish Catholic padres.

2. Answers may vary and may include: it was risky for Tuhuy to put himself in such a prominent position, because he will be blamed if anything goes wrong; or that it was wise to try to control how the rest of the Native laborers will be treated and where the people you care about will be placed within the rancho labor system.

3. Student responses will vary.

Chapter 6 Words to Know

whimpered: made low, feeble sounds expressing fear, pain, or discontent

skirted: went around or passed the edge of

trek: a long, arduous journey, especially one made on foot

vowed: promised

vast: immense; of very great extent or quantity

ranchero: the owner of a rancho

addressing: speaking to another person or group of people, usually in a formal way

dormitories: rooms in which several people sleep

simultaneously: at the same time

foreman: a worker who supervises and directs other workers

jefecito indio: "little Indian boss" - supervisor of the Indians

Chapter 7 – Vaqueros and Maid Servants
Questions

1. The job of *vaquero* was vital to rancho life. Describe the tasks and skills required of a *vaquero*.

2. In this chapter, Malik and Alapay become conflicted as they learn and master their new tasks on the *rancho*. Why are they conflicted? Explain an instance in which you have had conflicting thoughts.

Chapter 7 Answers

1. *Vaqueros* are skilled at:
   - riding a horse
   - creating and controlling a *reata* or lariat
   - roping and tying a calf or steer
   - rounding up and herding cattle
   - separating cattle
   - branding cattle

2. Malik is conflicted because he is proud to be successfully learning the skills of a *vaquero*; yet, these skills largely represent the culture Malik knows his father and uncle despise.

Alapay is conflicted because she has found an ally of sorts in Magdalena, the *ranchero's* daughter. As nice as Magdalena may be to her, Alapay knows she is merely a servant and that the other members of Magdalena's family do not share such a compassionate view of her or the other servants.

Student answers to personal experience will vary.

Chapter 7 Words to Know

trustee: a person who works for those in charge (in this case, the padres of the mission) and makes sure rules are followed

fortified: strengthened with defenses in order to prevent attack

forbidden: not allowed

Indio Jefe: another Spanish term for "boss of the Indians"

lasso: also known as a *reata* or lariat; a rope with a noose at one end steer: a neutered bovine male

eased: made something unpleasant less serious or severe

domestic: related to family or the running of a home

robust: strong and healthy

tyrant: a cruel and oppressive ruler

tedious: too long, slow, or dull; tiresome

compassion: sympathy, pity, and concern for the suffering or misfortune of others

inferior: lower in rank, status, or quality

condemnation: very strong disapproval

racial identity: a group of people who share a common history, nationality, or geographic area

Chapter 8 – The *Ranchero's* Daughter
Questions

1. If you were Diego, would you have agreed to help Kilik? Why or why not? What do you think motivated Diego to help him?

2. One may argue that some unethical (wrong, unfair) events take place in this chapter. Describe one of them and explain in what way(s) the event is unethical.

3. What evidence from this chapter supports the inference that Alapay is becoming as good a healer as her father?

Chapter 8 Answers

1. Student answers will vary, but may include the fact that the men have some similarities, in that both are considered outlaws. As a leader of a village of runaways, one might infer that Diego has just as much hatred for the invaders as Kilik does.

2. Student answers may include:
   - Señora Pacheco's treatment of Alapay; the woman made references to Alapay being uncivilized, a dirty Indian, and the reason why her daughter was sick.
   - The spirit of the land's choice to make Magdalena ill; she is an innocent child and treats the Native laborers nicely. She is not the reason why people suffer on this particular *rancho*.

3. Alapay is able to communicate with the spirits of illness and the spirits of the plants. She is able to identify the right plants to use as medicine. Although she has helped her father heal others in the past, she is able to heal Magdalena completely on her own.

Chapter 8 Words to Know

fortifications: defensive walls or other reinforcements built to strengthen a place against attack

irrelevant: not connected, applicable, or pertinent

summoned: urgently demanded for help

civilized: polite and well mannered

whisked: taken away suddenly and quickly

engulfed: surrounded or covered completely by (usually a natural force)

desecrate: to treat a sacred place or thing with violent disrespect impact: to have a strong effect on someone or something

scurried: moved hurriedly with short, quick steps

agony: extreme physical or mental suffering

meditative: involving meditation or concentrated thought

reverently: with deep and solemn respect

dramatically: greatly

Chapter 9 – The Bear and the Bull
Questions

1. If you were Malik, how would you have dealt with the unethical treatment of the bear?

2. What do Malik's actions in this chapter tell you about his character? In what way(s) is he similar to his father, Kilik?

Answers

1. Student answers will vary.

2. Student answers will vary, but may include: Malik cares about animals; he believes, as the Chumash do, that bears should be honored and respected. So, like his father, he follows traditional Chumash ways. He knows the bear song and uses it as Kilik once did. He also appears to sometimes act without thinking, as Kilik did when he was younger.

Chapter 9 Words to Know

ignorant: uneducated or unsophisticated

savage: a primitive and uncivilized person; considered a negative term for Native people

pivoting: spinning or rotating

bellowing: emitting a deep, loud roar

gruesome: causing horror

Indio tonto: Spanish for "Indian fool"

gawkers: people who stare openly at something or someone

tormented: experienced severe mental and/or physical suffering

timidly: shyly; in a way that shows lack of courage or confidence

sauntered: walked in a slow, relaxed manner, without hurry or effort

Que tonto eres: Spanish for "What a fool you are."

predicament: a difficult, unpleasant, or embarrassing situation

Vamonos, muchachos: Spanish for "Let's go, boys."

defy: to openly resist or refuse to obey

Chapter 10 – The Fiesta
Questions

1. Magdalena's parents make their opinions regarding her actions quite clear in this chapter. What is your point of view of Magdalena's behavior? What do her actions say about her character?

2. Tuhuy had to make a quick, difficult decision in this chapter. Do you think he made the right choice? What choice would you have made? Explain your reasoning.

3. Predict what Alapay will do next. What skills and character traits does she have that will assist her?

Answers

1. Student answers will vary but may include that Magdalena is brave to stand up for Malik and Tuhuy in front of her parents and all of their guests; she is foolish to think she can have any influence over her father.

2. Student answers will vary but may include that Tuhuy made the right decision because it would not have been right to hurt his own nephew; or Tuhuy made the wrong decision because he perhaps could have controlled the level of pain with which Malik had to suffer, and instead they both had to suffer at the hands of a cruel man.

3. Student predictions will vary but should include that Alapay has been taught by her uncle how to hunt and fight, and she also knows how to heal with plants. She knows the Samala Chumash language as well as some Spanish. She is kind and caring, as she took care of Magdalena; yet she is also determined.

Chapter 10 Words to Know

peasant: a poor person of low social status

garb: clothing or dress

devised: planned

sumptuous: splendid

acquaintances: people one knows only slightly, and who are not close friends

barbaric: savagely cruel; exceedingly brutal

spectators: people who watch an event

spectacle: something on display as unusual, notable, or entertaining

anticipation: a feeling of excitement about something that is going to happen

preposterous: utterly absurd or ridiculous

heathen: a term for someone who does not belong to a religion (usually a negative term)

sternly: in a serious or severe manner

sear: to burn (in this case, a figure of speech)

Chapter 11 – Free at Last
Questions

1. Where might 200 warriors have come from to assist Diego and Kilik in the attack?

2. Kilik has never been one afraid to take risks. Was it wise to sneak onto the rancho prior to the attack? Explain your reasoning. Was it wise to trust the first man Kilik approached with the attack plan? Explain your reasoning.

3. What does it mean for someone to do something "with a gleam in his eye"?

4. Malik and Tuhuy were in a well-guarded room. How do you think it came to be that they were released?

Chapter 11 Answers

1. Student answers will vary, but may include that the warriors were just like Kilik and Diego - former mission Indians who were able to avoid being captured and taken to a *rancho*, or had escaped. Some may have had family at that *rancho* and wanted revenge and/or to help their own families escape.

2. Student answers will vary, but may include that both acts were risky, yet paid off in the long run. Without his visit, the Natives would not have known what was happening and would not have been prepared in advance to assist in the fight. The man he approached could have told Esteban or Señor Pacheco, which would have ruined the plan and possibly hurt his family further; but instead, it helped to prepare the workers and gave Kilik valuable information, like where his son and cousin were being kept.

3. "With a gleam in his/her eye" is an idiom that describes a person's facial expression when he/she is happy, amused, or knows a secret.

4. Accept reasonable responses.

Chapter 11 Words to Know

potentially: with the possibility to develop or happen in the future

detected: discovered or identified

exploits: bold or daring feats

elated: extremely happy

envisioned: imagined; visualized

avenge: to inflict harm in return for injury or wrong against another

unjust: unfair

deliverance: the action of being rescued or set free

silhouetted: shown as a dark shape outlined against a lighter background

barrage: a concentrated artillery bombardment over a wide area

lunged: made a sudden forward movement with the body or a weapon

toppled: became unsteady and fell

ceased: stopped

clenched: pressed tightly together in anger, determination, or to suppress a strong emotion

Chapter 12 – The *Ranchero's* Revenge
Questions

1. Was it ethical for the Native laborers and servants to take the horses and all the food and tools they could when they left *Rancho Caballero*? Why or why not?

2. Summarize the events that take place once the Natives arrive at the Hidden Place.

3. If you were a former laborer or servant at *Rancho Caballero*, what would your mood be upon arriving at the Hidden Place? What might you say to Diego or Kilik?

4. Why do you suppose Diego and Kilik stayed at the Hidden Place and prepared for another battle instead of leading everyone in the village to another place of safety?

5. This chapter is entitled "The *Ranchero's* Revenge." What event takes place that proves this to be true? If you were Señor Pacheco, would your need for revenge be satisfied? What would be your next move?

Chapter 12 Answers

1. Student answers will vary, but may include that it was unethical because it is wrong to take what does not belong to you; it was ethical because Señor Pacheco never paid his servants or laborers for the work they did on his *rancho* even though he had promised to do so.

2. Events should be similar to:
   - Alapay doctors Malik and Tuhuy
   - Kilik brings the survivors from the Place of Condors to the Hidden Place
   - What remains of Kilik and Tuhuy's families reunite
   - Mexican troops arrive, fight, and retreat
   - Repairs and reinforcements are made to the fortifications
   - Alapay heals Tuhuy in the sweathouse
   - Tuhuy and Kilik reconnect

3. Student answers will vary, but may include relief, happiness, anxious anticipation, or even sadness and anger if he/she was injured or lost a loved one upon leaving the rancho. Accept reasonable, thoughtful responses to the second question.

4. Student answers will vary, but may include that Kilik knew his son and cousin had not healed enough for further travel; Diego and Kilik were confident that their preparations were sufficient to survive and succeed another attack; Diego and Kilik wanted their own revenge.

5. The Mexican troops arriving to attack and kill the Natives were to be Señor Pacheco's revenge. Since they retreated, students may respond that Señor Pacheco will not be satisfied and will indeed send more troops next time. Accept reasonable responses.

Chapter 12 Words to Know

obtain: get, acquire, or secure

seized: took hold of suddenly and forcibly

impending: about to happen

siege: a military operation in which enemy forces surround an area and cut off supplies, in the hopes to force the surrender of those inside

caravan: a group of people traveling together

wielded: held and used

Chapter 13 – The Final Showdown
Questions

1. What character traits might you add to your description of Alapay after her actions in this chapter? Support your answer with evidence.

2. Provide some reasons why a Native person might fight *with* the Mexican troops instead of against them, besides wanting to be on the "winning side."

3. Compare and contrast the feelings of the Mexican troops with those of the Native warriors in this "final showdown." Include the causes for each of the different feelings you list.

Chapter 13 Answers

1. Students answers will vary, but may include that Alapay is brave to go into battle not only once, but twice; she is a bit reckless for calling out and letting the enemy know where she was hiding (perhaps taking after her uncle a bit); she is a skilled warrior, as she succeeded in wounding the enemy and not getting hurt herself.

2. Student answers will vary, but may include that perhaps the Native person has lost his/her entire family and/or has no village to return to; the *ranchero* for whom he/she works is kind and treats him/her well; he/she was offered a good reward for agreeing to fight against these "rebels"; he/she was forced to fight against them.

3. The Mexican troops as well as the Native warriors may have felt confident, scared, nervous, anxious, or worried at the beginning before the battle started, not knowing what the outcome would be for themselves or their side. The Mexican troops may have started feeling frustrated or shocked when they found that the Native warriors were so well prepared and appeared to be fighting with the sort of military tactics with which they were trained. This may have turned into fear, disappointment, or anger as the Mexican troops recognized defeat and had to retreat. The Native warriors may have felt pride, elation, and relief as they realized they won, and later sadness and grief if they found they had lost a loved one or friend in the battle.

Chapter 13 Words to Know

adrenaline: a hormone released in your body in times of stress, causing increased breathing and blood flow

contingent: a group of people

platoon: a group of soldiers usually led by a lieutenant

projectiles: objects propelled through the air, usually thrown as weapons

maneuvers: movements requiring skill (in this case military) and care

renegades: people who behave in rebellious, unexpected ways

bugle: a brass instrument like a small trumpet without keys, used for military signals

Chapter 14 – An Uncertain Future
Questions

1. Why are Solomol's use of the phrases "The flood gates have been thrown wide open" and "...ocean of strangers" good ways to describe the manner in which Europeans arrived onto the land now known as California?

2. Do you agree with the choice this family has made? Why or why not?

3. Can you predict the outcome of the journey they have chosen to take? What do you think will happen to the Native people staying behind at the Hidden Place?

4. What makes the events in this story important to California history? Use information from the story and your unit of study to explain your answer.

Answers

1. When real floodgates open, there's no stopping the rush of water that comes through, much like there was no stopping the arrival of Europeans onto Native land in California and elsewhere in North America. An ocean is vast and hard to measure, much like the numbers of Europeans arriving on the continent.

2. Student opinions will vary but should include good reasoning.

3. Predictions will vary. Encourage students to use evidence from the text and their own knowledge of the rancho period and California history to make reasonable predictions and support their answers.

4. Student opinions will vary, but may include that the events mark the transition of control over the lands in California from the Spanish to Mexican governments, the continuing and lasting effects of the mission system and Spanish colonizers on the land and Native people (disease, loss of language, loss of traditional plant and animal resources, land acquisition), the continuance of many of these practices under Mexican control, the destruction of Native culture (or at least the necessity to hide it in order to survive).

Chapter 14 Words to Know

lurked: waited in a hidden or distant place in order to do something harmful (used figuratively in this case)

temporary: lasting for a limited period of time; not permanent

inconvenience: a disruption to one's comfort

staunch: loyal and committed

descendants: people descended from a particular ancestor

nestled: situated in a half-hidden position

conflict: a serious disagreement or argument

Lands of Our Ancestors Book Two
Student Projects

The following suggested projects and activities will extend the learning of early California history across the curriculum. Each project meets at least one of the fourth grade History-Social Science Content Standards in section 4.2:

"Students describe the social, political, cultural, and economic life and interactions among people of California from the pre-Columbian societies to the Spanish mission and Mexican rancho periods."

The projects are appropriate for individual students, partners, or small groups. Completed projects can be presented to the entire class for shared learning. All materials needed for the projects are basic classroom and school supplies. Laptops, notebooks, and the school library are resources the students will also need.

*PLEASE NOTE:

Some of the Student Projects listed here are easily adaptable for use with other of the three Lands of our Ancestors novels. And likewise, some of the Student Projects suggested for the other two novels can be adapted for use with Book 2.

Projects and Activities

1. Recording History (Standards 4.2.5 and 4.2.8)

Primary sources are important resources to use when researching the past. In this activity, the student(s) will imagine that he/she is living in the 1800s and has been sent by the Mexican government to visit several prominent ranchos and record the sights and sounds of California.

2. Journal Project: The student(s) will:
- write journal entries, using appropriate dates, describing what he/she sees, eats, how he/she travels, his/her impressions of the ranchos, and the people he/she meets.
- describe the relationships among the rancheros, vaqueros or soldiers, and Native people.
- include drawings of rancho life
- use previous knowledge and new research to complete the project.

Materials: Paper, pencils, markers, colored pencils, laptops, copy of the story, resource books

3. Timeline Project: The student(s) will:
- create a timeline of the book from the escape to the journey out of the Hidden Place
- use resources to research important facts and dates to post on the timeline.
- use drawings, photos, or other pictures to illustrate the timeline.
- display the timeline in the classroom.

Materials: Butcher paper, colored pencils, markers, paints, glue, laptop, copy of the story, resource books

4. The Land (Standards 4.2.5, 4.2.6, 4.2.8)

The respect that the Native people in Lands of Our Ancestors have for the land continues in Book 2 despite continued loss of access to their traditional homelands. Throughout this book, several locations become new, temporary homes for the main characters.

5. Map Project: The student(s) will use the information from the story to create detailed visual representations of each of the following settings, including annotations on post-its or index cards which describe the significance of each part of the visual representation to the story:

- The Place of Condors (map or drawing)
- Rancho Caballero (diseño*)
- The Hidden Place (map or drawing)

Materials: Large construction paper or butcher paper, post-its or index cards, markers, colored pencils, paints, copies of the story

Note: a diseño is a map of the land required by the Mexican government in order to acquire a land grant; images are available in most social studies curricula and can also be found on the internet under "rancho diseño."

6. Acquiring Knowledge (Standards 4.2.5, 4.2.7, 4.2.8)

Fact Box Project: This game activity reinforces new material learned in the unit of study and will motivate students to research additional information.

The student(s) will cover and decorate a shoe box or similar size box. Decorations should illustrate one of the story themes or scenes. There should be an opening at the top of the box large enough to reach inside. Using index cards, the student will write 15 or more question cards about daily life for Native and non-Native people on the *ranchos*. Answers to the questions should be written on the back of the question cards. Questions can be true or false.

Examples:

Q: Who made the adobe bricks for the rancho buildings?
A: The Native men and boys made the adobe bricks.

Q: True or False? Missions and ranchos had the same purpose.
A: False

Students can play the game one-on-one or in teams, taking turns choosing cards from the box. Students can decide if they want to keep score; awarding points for correct answers or even designating different point values per question based on the difficulty of each.

Materials: Shoe box, paper, scissors, tape, colored pencils, markers, index cards, laptop, resource books, copy of story

7. Compare and Contrast (Standard 4.2.5)

Poster Project: Student(s) will make three posters to be displayed side by side. Each poster will represent a different group: Natives, *vaqueros*, and soldiers. Students will use words and pictures to illustrate each group's daily life. The side by side display will illustrate the contrast. This project can include an oral presentation or explanation of the information in the posters and students' opinions.

Materials: Poster board, markers, colored pencils, drawings or pictures, glue, laptop, resource books, copy of story

8. Plants and Animals (Standard 4.2.6, 4.2.7, 4.2.8)

Many of the plants and animals native to the area known as Alta California became threatened when Europeans arrived in large numbers and brought animals and seeds with them. In fact, there is evidence of non-native, otherwise known as invasive, plants within the old adobe bricks used to build the missions. These invasive plants forever changed the hunting and gathering traditions of California Native peoples and thus, their diet, their medicines, their traditions, their culture.

Further destruction of the land continued through the establishment of mission agriculture and later, the ranchos.

9. Mini Display Board Project

Student(s) will research native plants and animals and how they were traditionally used by California Native peoples. Student(s) will also research the invasive plants and animals brought by Europeans and how these non-native species affected the land and Native people who depended on it.

The Mini Display Board will be created using file folders and post-its, allowing the student(s) to include information both on and underneath each post-it. The format may be by the categories listed above, using a compare and contrast organizational structure, or, if research lends itself, using a cause and effect or food chain organizational structure.

Suggested native plants: dogbane, tule, willow, juncus, oak, elderberry, deergrass, yucca, agave, sage, milkweed, sumac, yerba mansa, soap root, manzanita, toyon

Suggested native animals: deer, tule elk, grizzly bear, rabbit, coyote, bobcat, birds of various kinds, mountain lion

Suggested invasive plants: barley, ryegrass, wild oats, curly dock, wild lettuce, wild mustard, spiny sowthistle, redstem filaree (all found in mission adobe bricks) (*students may also consider researching the effect of agriculture on native plants, ie. the vineyards, orchards, and crops like wheat, barley, corn, beans, and peas that were first grown in the missions*)

Suggested invasive animals: horses, cattle, sheep, goats, hogs

Materials: file folders, post-its, pencils, markers, colored pencils, pictures or drawings, laptops, copy of the story, resource books

Lands of our Ancestors Book Three Teacher's Guide

Developed by Fred Messecar
and Gary Robinson

Lands of Our Ancestors Book Three
Teacher's Guide Introduction

This Teacher's Guide is designed to enrich teaching <u>Lands of Our Ancestors Book Three</u> across the curriculum. After this introduction, the guide begins with the California Content Standards for 4th grade History-Social Sciences the book addresses. This will provide teachers with important information about what the focus should be in teaching the Mexican-American War, Gold Rush and Early Statehood periods.

Section Three contains Overviews of the periods addressed in Book Three. This is followed by a section that validates the accuracy of the events portrayed in <u>Book Three</u>. Section Five provides pages of Images of Life during the era. These images help illustrate the story for students. Because the characters relocate several times during the story, Section Six is a list of the main geographic locations of the book.

Next, the guide provides a list of additional sources of information about the Chumash people, the Gold Rush and Statehood, if needed, for further research.

The next section of the guide contains the same "Characters and Relationships" reference as well as the "Timeline" found in the book. Section ten, the largest section of this guide, contains "Questions, Answers, and Words to Know" for each chapter of <u>Book Three</u>. The questions can be used in teacher-directed class discussions, small group discussions, or as written work. The variety of questions in each chapter align with The Six Levels of Questioning: knowledge, comprehension, application, analysis, synthesis, evaluation. Answers are provided for all chapter questions. New vocabulary, including words from the Samala Chumash, other tribes, and Spanish languages, are found in each chapter's "Words to Know" section.

Near the end, to extend the learning after the book is completed, the guide includes possible project choices to engage students. The projects are designed to meet the needs of the diverse learners found in most classrooms. Each project meets a specific fourth grade History-Social Science Content Standard for California Public Schools.

Students who complete reading the story, discuss or write responses to the questions, and learn the new vocabulary words will meet a variety of the fourth grade California Common Core State Standards in reading, writing, and language.

California 4th Grade History Social-Science Standards

Students should be able to answer these questions:

- How did the discovery of gold change California?
- How did California become part of the United States?
- Why did people come to California?

4.3 Students explain the economic, social, and political life in California from the establishment of the Bear Flag Republic through the Mexican-American War, the Gold Rush, and the granting of statehood.

1. Identify the locations of Mexican settlements in California and those of other settlements, including Fort Ross and Sutter's Fort. [SEP]

2. Compare how and why people traveled to California and the routes they traveled (e.g., James Beckwourth, John Bidwell, John C. Fremont, Pio Pico). [SEP]

3. Analyze the effects of the Gold Rush on settlements, daily life, politics, and the physical environment (e.g., using biographies of John Sutter, Mariano Guadalupe Vallejo, Louise Clapp). [SEP]

4. Study the lives of women who helped build early California (e.g., Biddy Mason). [SEP]

5. Discuss how California became a state and how its new government differed from those during the Spanish and Mexican periods. [SEP]

We recommend also consulting the **California History Social Studies Framework** for additional background information. The framework focuses on the Gold Rush and Statehood beginning on page 77 of the PDF version, which can be found online at: https://www.cde.ca.gov/ci/hs/cf/documents/hssfwchapter7.pdf

California Common Core Language Arts Standards

Vocabulary:

- CCSS.ELA-LITERACY.L.4.4

Determine or clarify the meaning of unknown and multiple-meaning words and phrases based on grade 4 reading and content, choosing flexibly from a range of strategies.

- CCSS.ELA-LITERACY.L.4.6

Acquire and use accurately grade-appropriate general academic and domain-specific words and phrases, including those that signal precise actions, emotions, or states of being (e.g., quizzed, whined, stammered) and that are basic to a particular topic (e.g., *wildlife, conservation,* and *endangered* when discussing animal preservation).

Comprehension:

- CCSS.ELA-LITERACY.RL.4.1

Refer to details and examples in a text when explaining what the text says explicitly and when drawing inferences from the text.

- CCSS.ELA-LITERACY.RL.4.2

Determine a theme of a story, drama, or poem from details in the text; summarize the text.

- CCSS.ELA-LITERACY.RL.4.3

Describe in depth a character, setting, or event in a story or drama, drawing on specific details in the text (e.g., a character's thoughts, words, or actions).

Overview of the Mexican-American War, Gold Rush and Early Statehood

In the 1840s, more immigrants from the United States and other countries began to arrive in Alta California, and Mexico was having trouble maintaining control of the territory. At the same time, Mexico was also having territorial troubles in another region, Texas, as the United States aggressively sought to expand its own lands. This led to war between the U.S and Mexico.

The Mexican–American War took place from 1846 to 1848, but most of the fighting happened outside California. This war followed in the wake of the 1845 annexation of Texas by the U.S., after the Texas Revolution a decade earlier.

About the same time, troubles between American settlers and Mexicans in Alta California had begun in earnest. In June of 1846 a band of Americans revolted, took over the city of Sonoma and jailed the Mexican governor, Mariano Guadalupe Vallejo. They raised the "Bear Flag" for the first time in the state. Then, acting on information that the English and Russians were planning to move in, American Commodore John Drake Sloat anchored in Monterey, the capital of Alta California, and raised the American flag. Sloat and his crew met no resistance from those living in Monterey. Approximately one-third of the northern half of Mexico, including California, became part of the United States after the U.S. defeated Mexico in 1848.

Just as the war was ending, James Marshall, an employee of immigrant landowner John Sutter, discovered a little nugget of gold at Sutter's lumber mill on the American River in Coloma, California. News of the discovery spread like wildfire worldwide, bringing some 300,000 gold-seekers to the territory. The sudden influx of money and people allowed American settlers to quickly move toward statehood.

The effects of the Gold Rush were substantial. Whole indigenous societies were attacked, decimated and pushed off their ancient lands by gold-seekers, called "forty-niners" in reference to the peak year of the Gold Rush immigration, 1849. San Francisco was the primary arrival point for those coming by sea, and the sleepy seaside village morphed into a major metropolis within a few short years. Those traveling by land often came over the Sierra Nevada Mountains by stagecoach, wagon train and later, locomotive.

The Gold Rush also caused environmental destruction through the introduction of hydraulic mining in the 1850s, which clogged and polluted rivers throughout the state, at great cost to the farmers and Native American villages downstream.

In the political arena, in 1849, delegates from around California gathered in Monterey, then the capital, to write a constitution for the new state. That constitution copied substantial portions of constitutions of other states as well as the U.S. Constitution, but also contained original provisions. The new constitution was ratified by popular vote later that same year, and Congress made California the thirty-first state in September, 1850.

As settlers continued to flood the state, Native Americans continued to suffer. Native inhabitants were often forcibly removed from their tribal lands by incoming miners, ranchers and farmers. Additionally, more than three hundred massacres of California Indians were carried out, while disease and starvation also took heavy tolls.

The new state government encouraged the process by passing laws that stripped Indians of rights while enabling non-Indians to buy and sell Indians as laborers. California's first Governor, Peter Burnet, openly called for a "war of extermination" of indigenous peoples while the state legislature provided the means of funding militias to carry out this policy. Between 1850 and 1860, the state paid out around one and a half million dollars for "expeditions against Indians."

Sources: An American Genocide; Wikipedia; California History-Social Science Framework

Accuracy of Events Portrayed in <u>Lands of our Ancestors Book Three</u>

This work of historical fiction depicts what might have happened to California Native Americans as Alta California transitioned from Mexican control in the 1840s to US/American control in 1850 and beyond. Although the characters and the specific plot are fictional, the people and events in the book are based on historical documents and the historical writings of non-fiction authors and scholars.

More specifically, for example, some of the details of the lives of California Indians during the Gold Rush era came directly from the non-fiction personal narrative <u>Unwritten History: Life Among the Modocs</u>, written by Joaquin Miller and first published in 1873. Facts regarding the campaigns to slaughter California Natives from the end of the Mexican-American War to the early years of California statehood came from early California newspapers and <u>An American Genocide: The United States and the California Indian Catastrophe</u>, written by Benjamin Madley, published in 2016.

However the period is depicted, the truth is that the Gold Rush and the early years of California statehood contributed heavily to the further destruction and devastation of Native American peoples, communities and cultures in the region that became known as California.

Images of California Life
Mid 1840s - 1855

Larkin House, Monterey. Built three blocks from the bay in 1835 by American merchant Thomas Larkin. It was the first two-story house in Monterey. Larkin operated a store from the back of the house. This is where Alapay reconnected with her Mexican friend, Magdalena.

This is a typical horse-drawn cargo wagon like the ones described on page 36. These vehicles were the delivery trucks of their day.

Sutter's famous lumber mill at Coloma, CA, on the American River where gold flakes were discovered in January, 1848. Geological forces working over millions of years produced high concentrations of the metal in this region of California, which was the ancient homeland of the Nisenan Indian people.

Images of California Life
Mid 1840s - 1855, continued

Pictured to the left is a method of gold-mining known as sluicing. Water from a riverbed is diverted into the sluice, allowing miners to pan for gold in the river's dry gravel bed. Groups of miners maintained camps near rivers and streams, tearing down and rebuilding the sluices as they cleared all the gold from a section of the river.

This image portrays the hydraulic method of gold mining as depicted on page 128 of Lands of our Ancestors Book Three. Many of the methods of mining gold destroyed the environment and made it impossible for plants, animals and fish to survive nearby.

San Francisco, 1850. After the discovery of gold in Alta California, San Francisco was transformed from a sleeping little seaside village into a major international city within two years. It was the main arrival point for gold seekers traveling by sea from all over the world.

Images of California Life
Mid 1840s - 1855, continued

Single shot, muzzle-loading pistol like the ones captured by Kilik and the people of Tukuyun's village described in chapter four.

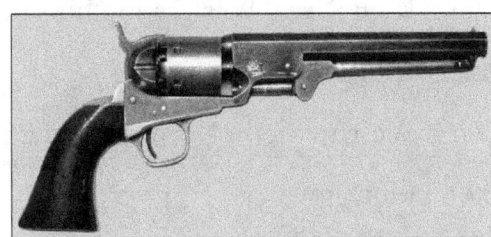

Colt 44 caliber revolver like the one Henry used to free Alapay on page 145. The single shot musket style pistol was no match for this innovation in weaponry.

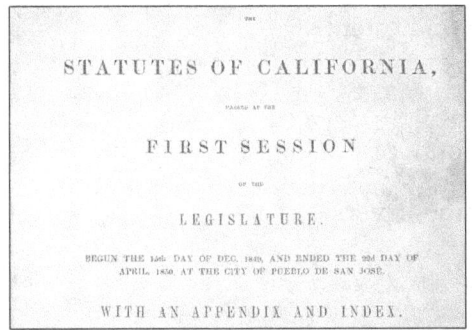

The newly created California state legislature wasted no time in passing laws that stripped Native Americans of their rights to land and liberty while giving other state citizens the ability to purchase Indians for labor.

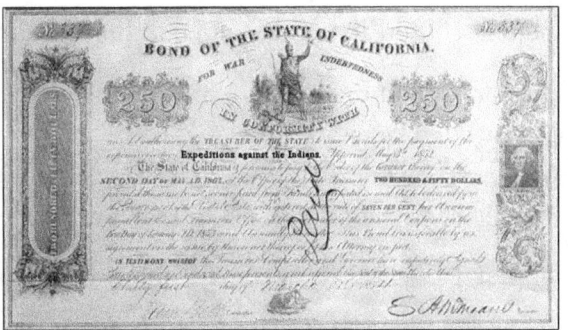

The new state government also provided the means to finance "Expeditions against the Indians" such as issuing bonds for sale to the public. This example bond had a value of $250. Around 1 million dollars was paid to militias that murdered thousands of California Indians.

These are the ruins of La Purisima Mission, which, like most of the Spanish missions, had been abandoned by the 1850s. As described on pages 171-174, Kilik's family passed by several mission ruins on their return journey to their homeland. A few California Indians somehow managed to miraculously survive the successive invasions of outsiders intent on taking the lands and resources of the area's original inhabitants.

Geographic Locations in Book Three

Chapter 1 Cuyama Valley, Southern San Joaquin Valley

Chapter 2 Kern River, Western foothills of the Sierra Nevada Mountains

Chapter 3 King River

Chapter 4 Western Sierra Nevada Mountains

Chapter 5 Monterey

Chapter 6 Monterey and surrounding ranchos

Chapter 8 Monterey and surrounding ranchos

Chapter 9 Monterey and surrounding ranchos

Chapter 10 San Joaquin Delta and its tributary river system

Chapter 11 San Francisco, American River

Chapter 12 South Fork of the American River; South of Folsom, CA

Chapter 13 Kosumme (Cosumnes) and Mokelumne Rivers

Chapter 14 Western Sierra Nevada Mountains

Chapter 15 Stockton, French Camp, Fresno

Chapter 16 Lake Tulare (now a dry lake bed), Mission San Luis Obispo, Mission La Purisima Concepcíon, Mission Santa Inez, and the Santa Ynez Valley

Sources on the Chumash People:

1. California's Chumash Indians, A Project of the Santa Barbara Museum of Natural History; EZ Nature Books; 1992, Revised Edition 2002.

2. The Chumash, Seafarers of the Pacific Coast; Karen Bush Gibson; Capstone Press, 2004.

3. "The Samala People" (DVD); produced by the Santa Ynez Band of Chumash Indians; Available from the tribe's Culture Department; 805-688-7997.

4. Bad Indians: A Tribal Memoir; Deborah A. Miranda; Heyday, 2013.

5. Samala-English Dictionary-A Guide to the Samala Language of the Ineseno Chumash People; Santa Ynez Band of Chumash Indians with Richard Applegate, PhD; 2007.

6. Website: www.sbnature.org/research/anthro/chumash/intro.htm (Chumash section of the Santa Barbara Museum of Natural History's website)

7. Website: www.santaynezchumash.org/history.html (The Santa Ynez Band of Chumash Indians official website)

8. Wikipedia Website: https://en.wikipedia.org/wiki/Chumash_people.

Sources on the Gold Rush and Statehood in California:

1. Unwritten History: Life Among the Modocs; Joaquin Miller; Orion Press, 1972; first printed 1873.

2. An American Genocide: The United States and the California Indian Catastrophe; Benjamin Madley; Yale University Press, 2016.

3. The Conflict Between the California Indian and the White Population; Sherburne F. Cook; University of California Press, 1976.

4. The Destruction of California Indians; Robert F. Heizer; University of Nebraska Press, 1974; republished by Bison Books, 1993.

Characters and Relationships in the <u>Lands of our Ancestors</u> series

Kilik (Miguel) – main character, son of Solomol and Wonono

Tuhuy (Rafael) – Kilik's cousin, son of Salapay and Yol

Stuk (Maria) – Kilik's younger sister

Solomol (Salvador) - Kilik's father

Salapay – Tuhuy's father

Wonono – Kilik's mother

Yol (Yolanda) – Tuhuy's mother

Tah-chi – Yokuts Indian scout for the Place of Condors village

Kai-ina – (Yokuts) Kilik's second wife, mother of Malik

Taya – Tuhuy's wife

Alapay (Andrea) – Tuhuy's daughter and Malik's cousin

Malik (Mateo) – Kilik's son and Andrea's cousin

Diego – Native outlaw and leader of Indians who attacked ranches

Magdalena Pacheco – Ranch owner's daughter who befriends Alapay

Limik – (Yokuts – Hawk) Kai-ina's father

Tukuyun – (Yokuts - Jackrabbit) Chief of one of the Yokuts bands

Loknee – (Miwok – Rain Falling Through) Chief of one of the Miwok bands

Mariposa – (Butterfly – Spanish) Miwok woman who marries Malik

Henry Jamieson – American newspaper reporter

Timeline of Historical and Fictional Events in the Lands of our Ancestors series

1769	First mission established in San Diego
1776	Solomol is born at the "Place of River Turtles" village
1777	Salapay is born at " " " " "
1780	Solomol's wife Wonono is born at the "Place of River Turtles" village
1781	Salapay's wife Yol is born at the "Place of River Turtles" village
1792	Kilik is born at " " " "
1793	Tuhuy is born at " " " "
1797	Kilik's sister Stuk is born at " " "
1804	Kilik & family go to mission
1804-05	Kilik & family experience hardships in the mission
1806	Children escape the mission on Summer Solstice morning (June)

Book 1 Ends

1806	Arrive at "Place of Condors" village
1811	Kilik marries Lau-lau (Yokuts) – Kilik is 19
1812	Earthquake damages missions in Chumash territory
	Baby is born to Kilik night of earthquake, but mom & baby die
1813	Stuk dies from measles brought to village by visitor
1814	Tuhuy leaves village to live alone, study healing, hermit
	Kilik leaves village to explore the region
1819	Kilik returns to village –
	Tuhuy returns to village, sees Taya (several years younger)
1820	Tuhuy marries Taya (Coastal Chumash) Tuhuy is 27
	Simultaneous ceremony: Kilik marries Kai-ina (Yokuts)
1821	Malik is born to Kilik who is 29 years old & Kai-ina
	Mexico wins independence
1822	'Alapay is born to Tuhuy and Taya

1823	Cousins Malik and 'Alapay play together
1824	Kilik begins raiding ranches and missions for cattle – age 32
1825-30	'Alapay blends healing and fighting as needed
1832	Kilik turns 40
1833	Tuhuy turns 40
1833	Kilik begins to train 12-year-old Malik as hunter & warrior
	'Alapay wants to learn too
	Spanish padres expelled from missions – Mission Indians released
	Pacheco gets major land grant – needs laborers
	Epidemic outbreak (flu)
1834-1848	Mexican Rancho Period
1834	Pacheco's men raid Condor Village; take Tuhuy and others to Ranch
	Tuhuy and everyone held at ranch, must work
	Kilik finds crippled father, brings him and aunt Yol back
	Kilik raids ranches, looks for family, considered outlaw by Ranchers
	Kilik and Deigo raid Rancho Caballero, rescue the Family
	Hidden Place is attacked twice by Mexican forces, but defeated
	The Family leaves Hidden Place village and heads northward

Book 2 Ends

1835-1840	The Family travels northward to escape further troubles
1840	Settle near Monterey, capital of California under Spain & Mexico
	Posing as a Mexican, Malik (Mateo) gets job as Vaquero
	Family realizes they must have Mexican last names
1842	Alapay (Andrea) miraculously reconnects with Magdalena who helps
	Alapay gets a job in Monterey and learns some English
1846	U.S. ship sails into Monterey Bay/ Malik and Alapay return to their village
1846-48	Mexican-American War; Mexico conquered

1848	War ends – Treaty signed / New Gov't set up in Monterey
	Gold discovered on Sutter's land
	Malik is 27 – 'Alapay is 26
	American miners begin displacing & attacking Indians
1849	Gold Rush / International mix of miners invade Northern CA
	San Francisco transforms from little village to international city
1850	State Constitution Convention
	CA becomes a state
	First state governor (Peter Burnett) declares a war of extermination on Indians, and bonds were issued to raise funds to pay for this extermination
	Act for the Governance & Protection of Indians passed (this act allowed for sale and indentured servitude of CA Indians)
1851-52	CA tribes sign 18 treaties with US that were never ratified
1853	Federal Gov't begins establishing military reservations where Indians could live in isolation and protection from the general population
1854	State capital moves to Sacramento
1855	Church gives back small portion of land to Samala Chumash
	Several Native families settle on this land
	Kilik is 63 years old/Solomol is 79
1856	Kilik's family returns to the Place of River Turtles
	Solomol dies and is buried at the Place of River Turtles
	Baby born to Mariposa
	Baby born to Alapay

Chapter Questions & Answers

Words to Know for Each Chapter

Chapter 1 - Wearing Disguises

Words to Know:

1. disguises- to modify the manner or appearance of (a person, for example) in order to prevent from being recognized.
2. Alta California (Spanish)- high or upper California
3. notorious- known widely and usually unfavorably.
4. destination- the place to which one is going or directed.
5. sour- having the characteristics of smelling of decay.
6. resentment- indignation or ill will stemming from a feeling of having been wronged or offended.
7. foreign- located away from one's native country.
8. mass- a large but nonspecific amount or number.
9. trenches- a long narrow ditch embanked with its own soil and used for concealment and protection in warfare.
10. yield- to give up (an advantage, for example) to another.
11. motley- having elements of great variety or incongruity.
12. intrusion- an inappropriate or unwelcome addition.
13. livestock- domestic animals, such as cattle or horses, raised for home use or for profit, especially on a farm.
14. meager- deficient in quantity, fullness, or extent; scanty.
15. conceal- to keep from being observed or discovered; hide.
16. passage- movement from one place to another.
17. talisman- an object marked with spiritual importance and believed to confer on its bearer supernatural powers or protection.
18. reverently- marked by, feeling, or expressing reverence.
19. outcropping- a portion of bedrock or other stratum protruding through the soil level.
20. caravan- a company of travelers journeying together, as across a desert or through hostile territory.
21. *Hola* (Spanish)- hello
22. *Señor* (Spanish)- sir

*Questions with Answers:

1. Why did Kilik, Tuhuy and their families leave the village known as the Hidden Place?
   - Mexican government/Mexican military knew where the village was located and they knew they would be attacked again.
2. What is the reason Kilik and Tuhuy's families go in a different direction than Diego and his group?
   - They decided to go north where Kai-ina's people were from and had heard it was safer.
3. What is the talisman that Kilik gives to Malik? Where did it come from, and why is it important to Malik?
   - Piece of antler with deer hide string (necklace).
   - Blessed by a ceremonial leader at the Place of River Turtles.
   - Given to Malik by his father Kilik who wore it all his life.
4. What disguises did the group wear to trick the caravan of Mexican merchants? Where did those disguises come from?
   - Clothing from the Mexicans.
   - Clothing was taken from the dead bodies who had attacked the Hidden Place.
5. What was missing and needed to complete the groups' disguises in case they came across more caravans?
   - Leather shoes.

Student answers will vary but should mention these key details in their responses. This is true for answers to all chapter questions throughout this guide.

Chapter 2 - A Home Among the Yokuts

Words to Know:

1. incident- a particular occurrence, especially one of minor importance.
2. devastated- to overwhelm; confound; stun.
3. introductions- the act or process of introducing or the state of being introduced.
4. astonishment- great surprise or amazement.
5. precede- to be in front of or prior to in order.
6. exploits- an act or deed, especially a brilliant or heroic one.
7. fascination- the capability of eliciting intense interest or of being very attractive.
8. momentarily- for a moment or an instant.
9. embrace- to clasp or hold close with the arms, usually as an expression of affection.
10. drought- a long period of abnormally low rainfall, especially one that adversely affects growing or living conditions.
11. consulting- to seek advice or information of.
12. relocate- to move to or establish in a new place.
13. concentration- the act or process of concentrating, especially the fixing of close, undivided attention.
14. inevitable- impossible to avoid or prevent; certain to happen.
15. destination- the place to which one is going or directed.
16. suspicious- arousing or apt to arouse suspicion; questionable.
17. impatient- unable to wait patiently or tolerate delay; restless.
18. faltered- to be unsteady in purpose or action, as from loss of courage or confidence; waver.
19. seize- To take by force; capture or conquer.
20. *Indios* (Spanish)- Indians, Native Americans
21. reins- two long narrow straps attached to each end of the bit of a bridle and used by a rider or driver to control a horse or other animal.

Questions with Answers:

1. What strange and wonderful connection did Kilik and Limik, Kai-ina's father, have?
    - Both of their names translate to hawk or falcon.

2. What natural features make the village, Place Above, such a safe place?
   - Long winding path that leads to a flat place that overlooks the valley below.
3. Why did the Native people from Place Above need to leave after years of relatively peaceful living?
   - Signs in the night sky warned of danger.
   - Sources of food and water were drying up.
4. As the group traveled northward, what signal meant danger? What signal meant it was safe?
   - Coyote wail meant danger.
   - Magpie warble meant all clear.
   - Hawk screech warned 1 or 2 people were coming.
5. Why, when meeting a caravan while traveling, did the groups' disguises not work this time?
   - The Mexican soldiers knew they were disguised Indians because they had no last names.

Chapter 3 - The Place of the Sun

Words to Know:

1. retrieving- to search for, find, and bring back
2. settlement- a newly colonized region.
3. trailing- to follow behind.
4. solstice- either of two times of the year when the sun is at its greatest angular distance from Earth's equator.
5. Summer Solstice- in the Northern Hemisphere, the summer solstice occurs about June 21 and is the longest day of the year.
6. Winter Solstice- in the Northern Hemisphere, the winter solstice occurs about December 21 and is the shortest day of the year.
7. scarcity- insufficiency of amount or supply; shortage.
8. surname- a name shared in common to identify the members of a family, as distinguished from each member's given name. Also called family name, last name.
9. corral- an enclosure for confining livestock.
10. retaliate- to do something in response to an action done to oneself or an associate, especially to attack or injure someone as a response to a hurtful action.

11. mete- to distribute or allot.
12. designated- to indicate or specify; point out.
13. procession- a group of persons, vehicles, or objects moving along in an orderly, formal manner.
14. pursued- to follow in an effort to overtake or capture; chase.
15. projectiles- a fired, thrown, or otherwise propelled object, such as a bullet, having no capacity for self-propulsion.
16. severed- to cut off (a part) from a whole.
17. abandoned- left behind, deserted; forsaken.
18. converged- to come together from different directions; meet.
19. shackles- a device, usually one of a pair connected to a chain that encircles the ankle or wrist of a prisoner or captive.
20. pouches- a small bag often closing with a drawstring and used especially for carrying loose items in one's pocket.
21. assortment- a collection of various kinds; a variety.

Chapter 3 Questions with Answers:

1. Limik knows the horses will be a valuable food source for his people. How do Kilik and Malik convince Limik the horses are more valuable alive?
   - They tell them they have learned to ride these animals and that they could be useful for scouting larger areas.
2. Why did the group take on surnames (last names)? Which surname did each family take and why?
   - This would complete their disguises as Mexicans.
   - Tuhuy took the name, Solares. Kilik took the name, De La Tierra.
3. Why did Kilik think it was necessary to attack the caravan Malik spotted? Why did Tukuyun not want to attack the caravan at first?
   - They wanted to free the Indian captives.
   - Tukuyun thought it was too dangerous and didn't want to lose men.
4. Why do you think the Natives were surprised and delighted to see firearms and ammunition even though they did not know how to use them?
   - Knew the firearms were powerful tools.
   - Kept the firearms from their enemies.

Chapter 4 - Musket Balls and Gunpowder
Words to Know:

1. extensive- large in extent, range, or amount.
2. absolute- not to be doubted or questioned; positive.
3. vigorously- Characterized by or done with force and energy.
4. *Si, senor, inmediatamente, senor* (Spanish)- Yes sir, immediately, sir
5. venison- the flesh of a deer used as food.
6. convinced- to cause (someone) by the use of argument or evidence to believe something or to take a course of action.
7. prejudiced- a judgment or opinion against something or someone formed unfairly or without knowledge of the facts.
8. ignorance- the condition of being uneducated, unaware, or uninformed.
9. *Tonto* (Spanish name given to captured Mexican)- fool or stupid
10. chatty- inclined to chat; friendly and talkative.
11. rambling- lengthy and digressive.
12. *vaquero* (Spanish)- cowboy
13. *rancho* (Spanish)- ranch
14. pitted- to set in direct opposition or competition.
15. captive- one, such as a prisoner of war, who is forcibly confined, subjugated, or enslaved.
16. translator- an interpreter.
17. frustration- the act of preventing the accomplishment or fulfillment of something.
18. musket rifle- a smoothbore, single-shot, shoulder gun used from the late 1500s through the early 1800s.
19. simultaneously- happening, existing, or done at the same time.
20. muzzle- the forward, discharging end of the barrel of a firearm.
21. glared- to stare fixedly and angrily.

Questions with Answers:

1. Why does Kilik demand the Mexican man give him his shoes?
    - He wants to complete his disguise.
2. Why did Kilik not want to kill the Mexican? What information could he have about the strangers that would be helpful to the Natives?
    - The prisoner would be able to tell them about the Mexican people and what they are doing in the region.

- He knows where the towns are located and how they move from one location to another.
3. What name is given to the stranger? Who suggests the name and why does he give it to the prisoner?
    - Solomol suggests calling him Tonto because the padres had called native people this when they didn't understand.
4. In what way will the prisoner help the Native people? Why is Malik chosen to work with the prisoner?
    - Answer questions about the strangers and show them how to use the firearms.
    - Malik was chosen to speak to the prisoner because he spoke Spanish
5. What was used as a target while the Natives learned how to use the firearms?
    - Tonto's hat.

Chapter 5 - The Monterey Plan

Words to Know:

1. impending- to be about to occur.
2. domestic- a household servant.
3. *Ay caramba!* (Spanish)- Oh no!
4. loincloth- A strip of cloth worn around the loins.
5. *Oh, Dios Mio!* (Spanish)- Oh, my goodness or oh, my god.
6. intuition- the faculty of knowing or understanding something without reasoning or proof.
7. intuitive- Of, relating to, or arising from intuition.
8. ailments- A physical or mental disorder, especially a mild illness.
9. bustling- Excited and often noisy activity; a stir.
10. gag- Something forced into or put over the mouth to prevent speaking or crying out.
11. *Ese Indio escapado!* (Spanish)- That Indian escaped!

Questions with Answers:

1. Why does Malik want to go to Monterey?
    - Malik missed being a vaquero and heard there were jobs there.

2. Alapay also wants to go to Monterey, what reason does she give her father, Tuhuy, for wanting to go live there?
   - Alapay enjoyed her job working in the house.
   - Alapay tells her father she will be learning about the strange new people
3. What did the cousins do with Tonto when they arrived in Monterey?
   - Dressed Tonto as a native, put him on a horse and sent the horse running through town.
4. How were the guns captured both useful and useless to the people at the Place of the Sun?
   - Helped make hunting easier.
   - Ran out of gunpowder and could no longer be used.

Chapter 6 - Mateo and Andrea

Words to Know:

1. lampposts- a post supporting a street lamp.
2. *Ingles* (Spanish)- English (language)
3. rounded- shaped into the form of a circle or sphere; made round.
4. embrace- to clasp or hold close with the arms, usually as an expression of affection.
5. *Rancho Buena Vista* (Spanish)- Good View Ranch
6. foreman- a man who serves as the leader of a work crew, as on a ranch or in a factory.
7. lasso- to catch, tie, or attach with or as if with a lasso.
8. riddled- to pierce with numerous holes; perforate.
9. plague- to cause suffering or hardship for.
10. fondness- having a strong liking, inclination, or affection.

Questions with Answers:

1. Why would Alapay and Malik, not know that Monterey is the capital of Alta California?
   - They have been living in a village far away.
   - They have never been there before.
2. What was Alapay's surprise when she went looking for work at Mr. Larkin's?
   - Her old friend Magdalena worked there.

3. Malik was not happy about his new job offer, why did he think he should take it anyway?
   - He would be valuable as a spy for his village.
4. What ceremony does Yol ask Tuhuy to perform? Why does Tuhuy have concerns about performing it?
   - Condor Vision ceremony.
   - He has not performed the ceremony in a long time and is worried it will not work.

Chapter 7 - The Cowboy and the Maid

Words to Know:

1. stooping- to bend forward and down from the waist or the middle of the back.
2. *Mariposa* (Malik's wife-Spanish)- butterfly
3. fateful- controlled by or as if by fate; predetermined.
4. marshes- an area of low-lying land that is usually saturated with water and is dominated by herbaceous rather than woody plants.
5. tributaries- a stream that flows into a larger stream or other body of water.
6. quarters- a place of residence, especially the buildings or barracks used to house military personnel or dependents.
7. mending- clothes and other articles that must be repaired.
8. phrases- a sequence of words that have meaning, especially when forming part of a sentence.
9. customs house- the office at a port or frontier where customs duty is collected.
10. wagers- a matter bet on; a gamble.
11. grove- a small wood or stand of trees lacking dense undergrowth.
12. expeditions- an outing undertaken with a definite objective
13. concluded- to bring to an end; close.
14. bolted- to move or spring suddenly.
15. cluster- a group of the same or similar elements gathered or occurring closely together; a bunch.
16. jockeying- to maneuver for a certain position or advantage.
17. trampled- to beat down with the feet so as to crush, bruise, or destroy; tramp on.
18. gasps- to draw in the breath sharply, as from shock.
19. spectators- an observer of an event, especially a sports contest.
20. beaming- to smile expansively.

Chapter 7 Questions with Answers:

1. What does Magdalena teach Alapay, and what does this allow her to do around town?
   - Teach her to read and understand a little English.
   - Read signs and posters.

2. What was the Native woman's name and why was Malik (Mateo) not supposed to talk to her?
   - Mariposa / Natives were not allowed to talk to Mexicans and Malik was pretending to be a Mexican vaquero.

3. What happened to Magdalena's father? Why did she leave her home?
   - After the Indians escaped he became more bitter and unforgiving.
   - She did not like being around him.

4. Why does Mateo (Malik) start off lagging in the race?
   - To avoid being pushed and shoved; trampled.

Chapter 8 - The Falcon Rides Again

Words to Know:

1. gobbling- to take greedily; grab.
2. citizenry- citizens considered as a group.
3. horsemanship- the skill of riding horses; equitation.
4. scanned- to look at carefully or thoroughly, especially in search of something; examine.
5. spurting- a sudden forcible gush or jet.
6. gazing- to look steadily, intently, and with fixed attention.
7. militias- an army composed of ordinary citizens rather than professional soldiers.
8. turmoil- a state of extreme confusion or agitation; commotion or tumult.
9. engulf- to swallow up or overwhelm by or as if by overflowing and enclosing.
10. aye- an affirmative vote, yes.
11. heathens- one who is regarded as irreligious, uncivilized, or unenlightened.
12. saddling- to put a saddle onto.
13. barbaric- marked by crudeness or lack of sophistication.

Chapter 8 Questions with Answers:

1. What problems did Native people face as the strangers spread out further across the countryside?
   - Gobbling up ancestral hunting and food gathering land.
2. During the raid at Rancho Buena Vista, why did Mateo have to fire his weapon?
   - So the vaqueros would not think he was one of the natives.
3. Why were Mexican militias formed? Were these militias fair? Why or why not?
   - Militias were formed to retaliate against raids.
   - Raids often did not seek justice; slaughtered any Natives they found.
4. Why are the rancheros going to raid Tukuyun's village? What does Mateo (Malik) know he must do?
   - Punishment for the raid.
   - Malik must leave and warn the village.
5. How does Mateo (Malik) convince Mariposa to leave with him?
   - Tells her he loves and wants to marry her.

Chapter 9 - New Rulers New Laws
Words to Know:

1. dismounted- to get down from a horse or other steed.
2. paste- a soft, smooth, thick mixture or material.
3. various- of diverse, different kinds.
4. uproot- to force to leave an accustomed or native location.
5. fortified- to strengthen and secure (a position) with fortifications.
6. refugees- one who flees, especially to another country, seeking refuge from war, political oppression, religious persecution, or a natural disaster.
7. vantage- a position, condition, or opportunity that is likely to provide superiority or an advantage.
8. flora- plants considered as a group, especially the plants of a particular country, region, or time.
9. fauna- animals, especially the animals of a particular region or period, considered as a group.
10. ligaments- a sheet or band of tough, fibrous tissue connecting bones or cartilages at a joint or supporting an organ.

11. sling- a weapon consisting of a looped strap in which a stone is whirled and then let fly.
12. arc- something shaped like a curve or arch.
13. anew- once more; again.
14. impact- to have an effect on.
15. nugget- a small, solid lump, especially of gold.
16. inhabitants- one that lives in a place, especially as a permanent resident.
17. legislature- an officially elected or otherwise selected body of people with the responsibility and power to make laws for a political unit, such as a state or nation.

Chapter 9 Questions with Answers:

1. Why is Malik concerned about his father?
   - He knew he was shot in the raid.
2. What problems did other Yokuts, who had already tried to move east, face?
   - Disease and draught have taken a toll on food sources.
3. Who does Mariposa think can help the villagers?
   - Her tribe, the Miwok.
4. What had changed since Mariposa had been away from her tribe? How could this be a problem for the travelers?
   - John Sutter, s Swiss immigrant, built a fortified settlement.
   - Made travel more dangerous.
5. Why was Tuhuy so delighted to meet Loknee?
   - Both of their names are Rain; Loknee means rain coming through, Tuhuy means rain.
6. How did Kilik adapt to fighting after his injury left him unable to shoot a bow?
   - He started to use a sling.
7. What did living among the Miwok people allow Tuhuy and Alapay to do?
   - They reconnected with nature and spiritual practices.
8. Name the law that allowed white settlers to kidnap, sell or enslave Native American people.
   - Act for the Government and Protection of Indians.

Chapter 10 - A War of Extermination

Words to Know:

1. mass murder- the deaths of many individuals.
2. fascinated- to capture and hold someone's interest and attention.
3. prompted- to give rise to; inspire.
4. ignorance- the condition of being uneducated, unaware, or uninformed.
5. civilized- showing evidence of moral and intellectual advancement; humane, ethical, and reasonable.
6. extermination- to get rid of by destroying completely.
7. extinct- no longer existing or living.
8. expenditure- the act or process of spending money.
9. frustrated- to cause feelings of discouragement, annoyance, or lack of fulfillment.
10. sloshed- to agitate in a liquid.
11. silt- a sedimentary material consisting of very fine particles intermediate in size between sand and clay.
12. strained- done with or marked by excessive effort; forced.

Questions with Answers:

1. Who was Henry Jamieson and why was he fascinated with indigenous people?
   - Newspaper reporter.
   - Fascinated with indigenous people that had lived for generations without ruining the land.
   - He didn't believe they are sub-humans like many others did.
2. What prejudiced views had Henry heard about Indians?
   - They will sneak up and rob you in your sleep.
   - They are untrustworthy.
3. Why does the newspaper editor tell Henry the newspaper will not print stories about how bad Indians were being treated?
   - Most readers wanted to hear about the booming economy because of gold.
4. How was Alapay able to understand what the white men who were hunting for gold were saying?
   - She had learned English from Magdalena while she stayed at Mr. Larkin's.
5. What happened to the white men?
   - There was a gun fight between two groups of white men.

Chapter 11- Death at Dawn

Words to Know:

1. murmur- a low, indistinct, continuous sound:
2. hostile- of, relating to, or characteristic of an enemy.
3. consulted- to seek advice or information of.
4. provisions- the act of making preparations for a possible or future event or situation.
5. hulls- the main body of various structures or other large vehicles, such as a tank, airship, or flying boat.
6. flee- to run away, as from trouble or danger.
7. ghastly- causing shock, revulsion, or horror; terrifying.
8. erupted- to develop suddenly.
9. cautiously- showing or practicing caution; careful.
10. saddlebags- a pair of pouches hanging across the back of a horse behind the saddle.

Questions with Answers:

1. Why did Malik and Alapay travel to neighboring tribes' villages?
   - They knew how to ride horses, making the trip faster.
   - Send word to neighboring tribes about the trouble the new white strangers have brought.
2. What is the big announcement Malik and Mariposa share with the village?
   - They will be having a child.
3. How does Malik know the attack on the village was by surprise?
   - The men died without weapons in their hands.
4. How does Alapay know this attack was done by the white strangers?
   - She called on her spirit helper to reveal what had happened
   - I mages began to appear to her of the events that took place
5. Why does Alapay and Malik attack Henry when they first meet?
   - They think he may be with the group that attacked the village.
6. What does Henry hope to learn from staying in Alapay and Malik's village?
   - He wants to record what the white men are doing in their native lands.

Chapter 12- Follow Orders

Words to Know:

1. gesturing- a motion of the limbs or body made to express or help express thought or to emphasize speech.
2. *vamanos* (Spanish)- Let's go
3. peering- to look intently, searchingly, or with difficulty.
4. belched- to expel gas noisily.
5. troughs- a long, narrow, generally shallow receptacle for holding water or feed for animals.
6. plunged- to dive, jump, or throw oneself.
7. Eureka- used to express triumph upon finding or discovering something.
8. echoed- repetition of a sound by reflection of sound waves from a surface.
9. vigilance- alert watchfulness.
10. flint- a very hard, fine-grained quartz that sparks when struck with steel.
11. wad- a small mass of soft material, often folded or rolled, used for padding, stuffing, or packing.
12. kindling- easily ignited material, such as dry sticks of wood, used to start a fire.
13. mischievous- playful in a naughty or teasing way.
14. banter- good-humored, playful, or teasing conversation.
15. dreaded- causing terror or fear.
16. thread- to make (one's way) cautiously through something.
17. brandished- to wave or flourish (something, often a weapon) in a menacing, defiant, or excited way.
18. stockade- a jail on a military base or an area to keep animals.

Questions with Answers:

1. What did Malik mean when he said, "I know I'm going to be sick", to Alapay?
    - He is teasing her because she likes Henry
2. What did Malik say to Henry that surprised Alapay?
    - Called him friend.
3. Why was the salmon Malik speared so particularly good?
    - They had been eating only dried food.
    - Fresh meal.
4. Where were the cousins when they noticed the faded images? Why was this important to Alapay?
    - The cousins were in a cave.

- The cave paintings reminded Alapay of Tuhuy teaching her Chumash symbols and their purpose.
5. How did the cousins know the men with soldier uniforms on were not Mexican?
    - They were white men.
    - Rode with a red and white triangular flag.
    - They wore blue uniforms.
6. Why are the cousins worried no one back in the village will believe what they have seen?
    - Hard for them to believe what they have seen with their own eyes.
    - Doesn't seem possible.

Chapter 13 - Pay Good Money

Words to Know:

1. massacre- the act or an instance of killing a large number of humans indiscriminately and cruelly.
2. wadded- to compress into a wad.
3. fascinating- possessing the power to charm or allure; captivating.
4. dispersed- to separate and move in different directions; scatter.
5. awkward- clumsily or unskillfully performed.
6. clumsy- lacking physical coordination, skill, or grace; awkward.
7. column- something resembling an architectural column in form.
8. welt- a lash or blow producing such a mark.
9. *Hablo solo Espanol* (Spanish)- I only speak Spanish.
10. squaw- offensive slang, a Native American woman, especially a wife.
11. bluffing- to engage in a false display of confidence or aggression in order to deceive or intimidate someone.
12. holster- a case of leather or similar material into which a pistol fits snugly and attaches to a belt, strap, or saddle so that it may be carried or transported.
13. revolver- a handgun having a revolving cylinder with several cartridge chambers that may be fired in succession.
14. scurried- to go with light running steps; scamper.

Chapter 13 Questions with Answers:

1. Why wouldn't the editor publish Henry's story? What did this cause Henry to do?
   - Said the readers would not be interested in it.
   - Henry quit his job to write the book he always wanted to write.
2. What does Tuhuy say about trusting a white man? What does Alapay say to change his mind?
   - You can't trust a white man.
   - Alapay tells her father she has met another nice white man like Mr. Larkin who was respectful to Indians.
3. How did Alapay know, without seeing, the camp was not Henry's?
   - She heard more than one voice.
   - Henry would be alone.
4. What does Henry tell the men to try and set Alapay free?
   - That she belongs to him because he paid for her.

Chapter 14 - Eyes of the Condor
Words to Know:

1. dumbfounded- to fill with astonishment and perplexity; confound.
2. *perdoname* (Spanish)- excuse me.
3. utmost- of the highest or greatest degree, amount, or intensity; most extreme.
4. admiration- a feeling of strong approval or delight with regard to someone or something.
5. speculate- to engage in a course of reasoning often based on inconclusive evidence; conjecture or theorize.
6. absorb- to learn; acquire.
7. jotting- a brief note or memorandum.
8. phases- a distinct stage of development.
9. verbalized- to express in words.
10. parallel- moving in the same direction at a fixed interval.
11. maneuvered- a movement or combination of movements involving skill and dexterity.
12. miraculously- of the nature of a miracle.

Chapter 14 Questions with Answers:

1. What greeting gestures by Henry were unfamiliar to the people in the village?
   - Handshake.
   - Kissing a woman's hand.
2. How is Henry a new source of information for the people in the village?
   - He is a white man.
   - He has lived in their cities and know of plan for further expansion.
3. Why doesn't Tuhuy use the Eye of the Condor ceremony to see if they can return to the Place of River Turtles?
   - He wasn't able to perform the ceremony last three times he tried.
4. How does Alapay begin to prepare for the Eye of the Condor ceremony?
   - The night before, stay quiet and focus her energy.
   - Day of, multiple cycles of prayer and song.
5. What did Alapay take with her for the ceremony?
   - Tule reed mat.
   - Basket water bottle.
6. How did Alapay recognize the Place of River Turtles during the ceremony?
   - Her father had described where the Place or River Turtles was located.

Chapter 15 - The Long Journey Home
Words to Know:

1. anxiously- uneasy and apprehensive about an uncertain event or matter; worried.
2. *timolokich* (Chumash)- a story.
3. *que bueno* (Spanish)- That's good or that's great.
4. slopes- a stretch of ground forming a natural or artificial incline.
5. ferries- a place where passengers or goods are transported across a body of water, such as a river or bay, by a ferryboat.
6. cowering- to cringe in fear.
7. volley- a simultaneous discharge of a number of bullets or other projectiles.
8. steed- a horse, especially a spirited one.
9. fluttering- to wave or flap rapidly in an irregular manner.

Chapter 15 Questions with Answers:

1. Why do Solomol and Yol want to return to their home village?
   - They are getting older and it would mean a lot to be able to see their old home.
2. Why does Henry's plan cause anger at first? Who convinces the elders to think about it?
   - His plan suggests they pretend to be his slaves.
   - Malik tells Kilik it will only be a story, *timolokich*, when they encounter Mexicans or Americans.
3. How will Henry's plan help the villagers as they travel?
   - Avoid conflicts with other travelers.
   - They will be able to take faster routes.
4. What made it possible, as Kilik said, for the travelers to have survived the outlaws attack?
   - Planning, preparation and practice.

Chapter 16 - The Place of River Turtles

Words to Know:

1. odyssey- an extended adventurous voyage or trip.
2. territory- an area of land; a region.
3. ruins- the state of being physically destroyed, collapsed, or decayed.
4. adobe- a building material consisting of clay mixed with straw or dung, fashioned into sun-dried bricks or used as mortar or plaster.
5. dilapidated- having fallen into a state of disrepair or deterioration, as through neglect; broken-down and shabby.
6. ravaged- to bring heavy destruction on; devastate.
7. decrepit- weakened, worn out, impaired, or broken down by old age, illness, or hard use.
8. raspy- rough; grating.
9. rubble- a loose mass of angular fragments of rock or masonry crumbled by natural or human forces.
10. *haku* (Chumash)- hello
11. *lo siento, no entiendo* (Spanish)- I'm sorry, I do not understand.
12. knoll- a small rounded hill or mound; a hillock.
13. prying- insistently or impertinently curious or inquisitive.

Chapter 16 Questions with Answers:

1. Why was Kai-ina able to guide them as they continued south?
   - Recognized landmarks from her time living with the Yokuts.
2. How do Solomol and Kilik respond when the padre offered to rent a room?
   - They said No, they wouldn't stay there if you paid them.
3. At the ruins of Mission Santa Ines, why does Solomol want to go inside? Once inside, why does he make an offering?
   - It makes his heart feel good to see it in ruins.
   - Offers a blessing song for the hundreds of Chumash who are buried there.
4. Why was the offering at the mission so important to the group?
   - Began a small bit of healing.
5. Why didn't the native people they encountered speak their native languages?
   - After living at the missions so long no one knew the language anymore.
6. What happened to Henry and why didn't Alapay leave with him?
   - Spent several months writing his book about the Native people.
   - Asked Alapay to go with him; She said no, her place was with her people.

Language Arts/ History/ Social Science
Extension Projects and Activities

The following activities are suggestions for further learning and can deepen the connection between the narrative and real historical events in California's History. Attached to each suggested activity are some basic California learning standards for referencing.

- **Comic Strip Story Map**
  The elements of a story assist students in their understanding of what is taking place in the novel. When students comprehend the story elements of characters, setting, problems, events, and solutions, they become more involved in the story and take a greater interest. In this lesson, students use a 12-panel comic strip to create a story map. The story strips that result provide a great way to evaluate student's understanding of important events and elements in a novel.

  (Materials needed: construction paper, colored pencils/ markers/crayons, scissors, glue)

  -Common Core ELA Standards: CCSS.ELA-LITERACY.RL.4.1 CCSS.ELA-LITERACY.W.4.4

- **Triangle Diorama: The Four Basic Elements of a Story**
  A simple yet effective way to check for basic elemental understanding of a story. As a whole group, students will discuss the elements of the story prior to beginning the activity. Project should feature their understanding of story elements as well as present their creative interpretation. *Triangle diorama project instructions can be found online.*

  - Students represent four story elements, one per triangle diorama, creating a full square art piece representing student learning. (Plot, Characters, Setting, Theme)
  - Student art should be open to the student's interpretation of the story element being represented.
  - Attach student writing to the bottom of each triangle. Student writing should demonstrate understanding of the story elements in connection with the story and include an explanation of their art.

- (Materials needed: construction paper, colored pencils/ markers/crayons, scissors, glue)

-Common Core ELA Standards: CCSS.ELA-LITERACY.RL.4.2, CCSS.ELA-LITERACY.RL.4.3

- **Mapping the characters journey throughout California**.
  As the story is either read whole class or individually, come back as a group and discuss the routes taken by the lead characters. Using a large classroom map or individual electronic devices, plot the journey and discuss what hardships might be found, in not only the terrain, but also the resources.
  (Materials needed: Large classroom map or individual electronic devices)
  - On a large classroom map, have students plot California locations as characters travel throughout the state. *Technology Variation: Track locations on an internet-based mapping program.
  - Plot major Mexican and American Cities and settlements mentioned in the story.
  - Discuss routes taken by the story characters to elude detection and the major roadways used by the Mexicans and Americans. What made these routes possible? Which are still in use to this day?
  - Discuss the flora and fauna of each region. Students create flip books highlighting key features of each region. *Technology Variation: Students create interactive notes using a web-based slideshow program. Each slide can contain anything valuable to the student pertaining to a particular region including notes, pictures, video and links.
  - Discuss the Native regions and homelands as the characters move in and out of neighboring tribal lands. Students create flip books highlighting key features of home construction and clothing. *Technology Variation: Students create interactive notes using a web-based slideshow program. Each slide can contain anything valuable to the student pertaining to a particular region including notes, pictures, video and links.

-History-Social Science Content Standards: 4.1.5; 4.2.1; 4.3.1; 4.3.2

- **Journal Writing**
    - Alapay found great power in the ability to read, and Henry wanted his words to inform; our future needs to know this value.
        - Have students take on the role of Alapay. How is Alapay constantly learning throughout the story? What value do they see in keeping traditions going from one generation to the next?
        - Have the students take on the role of Henry. What do they want to tell the world about these native people they have been learning about? What value do they see in preserving this culture that was once threatened by extinction?

-Common Core ELA Standards: CCSS.ELA-LITERACY.W.4.1, CCSS.ELA-LITERACY.W.4.2, CCSS.ELA-LITERACY.W.4.3

Lands of our Ancestors author note:

My deepest and sincerest thanks go out to the three educators who developed the educational core of these teacher's guides: Cathleen Chilcote Wallac, Dessa Drake and Fred Messecar.

--Gary Robinson

www.ingramcontent.com/pod-product-compliance
Lightning Source LLC
Chambersburg PA
CBHW081400070526
44583CB00020B/2608